SIX DAYS—and SUNDAY

SIX DAYS—and SUNDAY

A PEW-PULPIT DIALOGUE

Dow Kirkpatrick

ABINGDON PRESS

NASHVILLE AND NEW YORK

SIX DAYS—AND SUNDAY

Copyright © 1968 by Abingdon Press

Library of Congress Catalog Card Number: 68-17439

SET UP, PRINTED, AND BOUND BY THE
PARTHENON PRESS, AT NASHVILLE,
TENNESSEE, UNITED STATES OF AMERICA

FOREWORD

I live in an ivory tower. I am a preacher.

There have been times when I thought I wanted to break down the walls and enter the layman's world, but I've never figured out how. This frustration has taught me a very happy lesson: I can't be someone else. I live where I live because I am who I am.

I can meet other people. When I listen to them talk about their worlds, I discover *everyone* lives in a tower of his own kind. Because I'm a preacher, I can't live in the world of the advertising man. It is just as true that because he is in advertising, he can't live in the world of the preacher.

So we each have something that the other doesn't have. We need, not to escape our world for some kind of inauthentic entrance into another, but we need each other. This, then, is the time and place to describe a method for meeting. It is not easy to have an original idea. We are so entangled in influences from others that ideas seldom, if ever, arise from only one mind. This one grew out of reading. The idea became the basis for a very meaningful series of dialogues in the study and the pulpit of the First Methodist Church, Evanston, Illinois. The dialogues were between laymen and the preacher, between pew and pulpit—between Sunday and the other six days.

SIX DAYS—and SUNDAY exactly expresses the purpose of the series: to make the Christian connection between the six days and the seventh. A small group of laymen in a specific vocation were invited to two sessions with the preacher before any preparation of the sermon was begun. They were asked to give some thought ahead of time, even to do some writing, so that when we came together in the first session we could list and describe the issues which confront them in their six-day world. These are the places where they want their Christian faith to help them.

Between the first and second sessions the preacher tried to coordinate these issues into an outline. That outline became the basis of the second discussion. This time Bibles were in hand. We tried to find direction from Scripture and the Christian faith in confronting these daily issues.

This small group was then asked to select one of its members as spokeman. This person wrote a letter (preferably on his own professional letterhead) to all members of the church known to be in the same profession, telling them of the Sunday when their vocation would be the basis of the sermon. On that day, the spokesman

6

entered the pulpit with the preacher. He was in the processional with the ministers. He spoke from the pulpit—not the lectern. He was without robe. These little bits of "stage business" are debatable, but they seemed right to us.

The layman was asked to make a five-minute statement carefully delineating the issues. The sermon followed, and after it a "pew-to-pulpit" session was held. This discussion could, in some churches, be held in the sanctuary itself. In our case it seemed desirable to go, after the benediction, to another room. The format of this book seeks to reproduce this process of dialogue by publishing the outline roughly drawn out of the first conversations, the more carefully prepared statement made by the layman from the pulpit, and the sermon. The experience has been one of very real meaning for this congregation. There are side benefits, such as the camaraderie which developed in several of the small groups of persons in the same profession, members of the same church. Many of them had not even known one another prior to this experience. To have been introduced to each other in this way is, I believe, one of the finer meanings of the Christian *koinonia*.

Another interesting evidence of the depth of involvement of the whole congregation in the process was the number of rather strongly worded complaints from people whose line had been left out! These were anticipated. The preacher would have been disappointed if no one had cared that his profession was seemingly neglected. These complaints provided the base for future preaching plans.

Other dialogues can result from this process. Sessions can be held in which the small group of laymen who helped the preacher are brought together with young people of the congregation interested in their vocational areas. An evening's discussion of this kind, in the home of the preacher or of one of the laymen, will again add a richness to the life of laywitness in the total congregation.

Best of all, I testify, is what such a process has done for the preacher. Two things of which I am certain: (1) The strength and integrity which is demanded of a layman who would be a Christian in his world is awesome. I do not speak of other ministers, but I have no confidence that I have moral fiber enough to live in their world. Maybe this is why God made me a preacher. He knows my soul needs the protections available in my world, not available in theirs. (2) I have been deeply moved by the kinds of persons who worship in our pews. Such stature—stature of faith and commitment, that is! We sometimes boast of the caliber of people who make up our congregations, especially one like First Church, Evanston. By which we have meant that they are powerful in the world in the things of the world. In these weeks of dialogue, again I have been taught what true Christian stature is and how abundantly we are blessed with it.

A word of caution to preachers: If you decide to do something like this, allow extra time for sermon preparation. These are not easy sermons to write. I now know how it must feel to be a poet laureate—that is, to be required to compose poetry for specific occasions!

Dow Kirkpatrick

Evanston
1968

With Gratitude
   to the community
   and these, the representatives of the
      community

"A sermon, therefore, must spring from more than the individuality of the preacher, the one particular man who happens to be speaking. A sermon must come from the community." (Rudolf Bohren, *Preaching and Community,* p. 51)

Those in Communications
      Hal F. Wierwill, Advertising Consultant
         Richard C. Art, Director of Media, Geyer, Oswald, Inc., Chicago
         Charles A. Sengstock, Jr., Director of Marketing, Soiltest, Inc.
         Dean Milburn, Vice-President and Sales Manager, Edwards and Deutsch Lithographing Co.
         Eugene E. Blackwell, Metropolitan Sunday Newspapers
         Mrs. Dorothy Millikan, Associate Editor, Rand McNally and Co.

Those in Medicine

> William P. Swisher, M.D., Internist and Teacher
> Earl O. Latimer, M.D., Surgeon
> John M. Bailey, M.D., Practicing Obstetrician and Gynecologist
> John L. Savage, M.D., Surgeon
> Melvyn A. Bayly, M.D., Professor, Obstetrics and Gynecology, Northwestern University Medical School

Those in Law

> John D. Hastings, General Attorney, Household Finance Corporation
> Harold Smith, Winston, Strawn, Smith & Patterson
> Marion E. Burks, Attorney, Estate Planning, Probate and Corporation Law
> James A. Rahl, Law Professor, Northwestern University
> Gwynne E. Old, Associate, Vinson, Elkins, Weems and Searls, Houston, Texas

Those in Business

> Dwight L. Myers, Regional Manager, Swan Rubber Company
> Gordon W. Campbell, Vice-President and Cashier, State National Bank
> Frank B. Palmer, Salesman, CBS Television Network
> Donald C. Malmquist, Vice-President, John Nuveen and Co.

Warren L. Lofgren, Owner, Warren Lofgren and Company

Frank Breckenridge, Vice-President and General Manager, Controls Company of America

Those in the Ministry

Charles M. ("Sandy") Huss, Jr., Ministerial Student, licensed to preach

Don A. Cooke, General Secretary and Treasurer, Council on World Service and Finance, The Methodist Church

Claire C. Hoyt, General Secretary, General Board of Pensions, The Methodist Church

J. Ralph Magee, Bishop of The Methodist Church

A. Turley Stephenson, Retired Methodist Minister

Horace G. Smith, President Emeritus, Garrett Theological Seminary

Herbert Scott, Retired Methodist Minister

Thomas A. Stafford, General Secretary Emeritus, General Board of Pensions, The Methodist Church

Herbert A. Keck, Retired Methodist Minister

Elliott Fisher (deceased), General Secretary, Commission on Promotion and Cultivation, The Methodist Church

Thomas B. Lugg (deceased), General Secretary and Treasurer Emeritus, Council on World Service and Finance, The Methodist Church

Those in Science

Charles A. Berry, Neuropharmacologist, Northwestern University Medical School

James E. Van Ness, Professor of Electrical Engineering, Northwestern University

Ariel G. Schrodt, Scientific Director, Packard Instrument Company

Stanley C. Harris, Professor and Chairman, Department of Pharmacology, Director, Division of Advanced Dental Education, University of Pennsylvania

Ernest H. Wakefield, President, Linear Alpha, Inc.

Johannes Weertman, Materials Science Department, Northwestern University

Those in Public Service

Armon Lund, Village Manager, Wilmette, Illinois

William A. Nott, Alderman, Evanston City Council

Harold D. Patterson, School Administrator

Connie Fish, Social Welfare Consultant, Welfare Council of Metropolitan Chicago

Those in the Dialogue on Women

Mrs. J. Robert Gettel, Mother of three; previously Teacher of Languages, Sweet Briar College and Roycemore School

Mrs. Erskine M. Jeffords, Wife of Methodist Minister; previously Secretary in industry and church

14

Mrs. James Kittleman, Mother of three

Mrs. Eugene E. Blackwell, Mother of four

Mrs. Marshall R. Barksdale, Mother of two; previously elementary school Teacher

Marguerite Stitt Church, Representative in United States Congress, 1951-63, and Delegate to United Nations, 1961

Those in Retirement

Arthur L. Myers, Retired Industrialist

William E. Jones, Retired, Chairman Science Faculty, Evanston Township High School

Milton W. Bollman, Retired Principal, Oakton School

H. W. Kirchhoff, President, Evanston Friendship Club

Mrs. W. Scott Robinson, Widow, Retired Principal of elementary school

"Since the Reformation the sermon, . . . has been without doubt the centre, the authentic heart of the Church. . . . But it is precisely here that today the crisis of the Church is most evident—as a crisis of preaching. . . . This Word is a word spoken from fellowship calling into fellowship. . . . For this reason it can be made intelligible only by, on the one hand, taking man seriously in his confused search for himself, for personal integration, and, on the other hand, by being spoken out of a fellowship which becomes visible as such behind the preacher, and receives into itself the man who is seeking fellowship." (Emil Brunner, *The Christian Doctrine of the Church, Faith and the Consummation,* pp. 99, 101-102)

15

CONTENTS

Communications

Conversation Guide 19
Statement of the Issues by Hal F. Wierwill 22
Sermon: "Children in the Market-place"
by Dow Kirkpatrick 25

Medicine

Conversation Guide 35
Statement of the Issues by William P. Swisher,
M.D. 38
Sermon: "Dr. Jesus" by Dow Kirkpatrick 43

Law

Conversation Guide 55
Statement of the Issues by John D. Hastings ... 58
Sermon: "Sue for Your Shirt"
by Dow Kirkpatrick 60

Business

Conversation Guide 71
Statement of the Issues by Dwight L. Myers ... 74
Sermon: "Mammon Is My Boss"
by Dow Kirkpatrick 76

Ministry

Ministry: An Explanation 87
Statement of the Issues by Charles M.
("Sandy") Huss, Jr. 88
Sermon: "Absurdly We Do . . ."
by Dow Kirkpatrick 90

Science

Conversation Guide 98
Statement of the Issues by Charles A. Berry . . .100
Sermon: "As if . . . God's Spies"
by Dow Kirkpatrick 103

Public Service

Conversation Guide 113
Statement of the Issues by Armon Lund 115
Sermon: "At Your Service" by Dow Kirkpatrick . 117

Women

Conversation Guide 130
Statement of the Issues by Mrs. J. Robert Gettel . 133
Sermon: "The Proverbial Woman"
by Dow Kirkpatrick 135

Retirement

Conversation Guide 146
Statement of the Issues by Arthur L. Myers . . .148
Sermon: "The Shadow Goes Down Easily"
by Dow Kirkpatrick 150

COMMUNICATIONS

CONVERSATION GUIDE

The designation "communications" was given to the broad field represented generally as advertising, public relations, etc.

I. The Issues
   A. Recognize that most of these issues are not confined to this one profession.
   B. The issue of honesty is, however, highlighted in a special way because of the nature of this profession.
      1. Clients feel they have a right to determine the image they want to show of their product; the advertiser may see this as false.
      2. The competition for an account puts pressure on to shape the presentation according to standards which may be personally offensive.
         a. Kickbacks, fringe handouts.
         b. Different prices for identical services.
         c. Advertising agents holding ownership in advertising media and then favoring their media.
      3. The "structured truth"; the neglect to dis-

seminate damaging information.

4. The concern over "image" instead of "identity."

C. The issues of the integrity of the person.

1. Some employers make unreasonable work demands on their employees, forcing them to forego constructive church and community activities.

2. Very frequently rewards are given to an employee for being "one of the boys." All too often arrogance and "big front" are accepted as strength and sincerity, and kindness is taken for weakness.

3. Sincerity—often tempted to promise more than he knows he can deliver.

4. Maintaining the "climate" needed for the creative work of getting ideas when one is involved in the "jungle" aspects of conferences, presentations, etc.

5. Involved in accounts which are morally unacceptable personally—liquor, cigarettes, racial practices, war products, gambling, etc.

D. What responsibility does a company or the agency have for raising moral issues? How to do it without being judgmental (e.g. Kemper Insurance and alcoholism).

E. Does advertising shape standards and values for the nation, and what responsibilities does the individual Christian have for this?

II. Beginning Thoughts
   A. How a person determines the limits of his flexibility.
   B. How the performance of a daily job is related to how the person thinks of himself.
   C. How are standards and values set in our national life?
      1. Advertising's role in *shaping* them.
      2. Business' role in *"cashing in"* on them.
   D. How to maintain a "climate" is one's inner self in the presence of great pressures.
   E. The relation of the Christian concept of the Word and the advertising field.
III. Scripture to look at for direction
   Proverbs 12:19-22; 16:8; 21:6; 23:23
   Habakkuk 2:2 (The origin of Burma Shave ads!)
   John 1:14
   Romans 12
   I Corinthians 5:6-8
   II Corinthians 2:17
   Ephesians 4:25
   Philippians 3:19; 4:8
   James 3:3-18

STATEMENT OF THE ISSUES
by HAL F. WIERWILL

There were eight of us in the group Dr. Kirkpatrick called together to acquaint him with the issues in our daily work on which we call our Christian faith to speak—eight of us in various phases of the field of communications.

While all of us couldn't agree on all the issues, we all did agree that Dr. Kirkpatrick is a man of courage. He has to be. To begin this important and provocative series of sermons with the field of communications takes courage!

In the first place, the field is even difficult to define. "Communications" is an all-inclusive umbrella word. It covers those endeavors and those enterprises which have to do with *informing* the public and *convincing* the public. Its focus is commercial; its techniques border on —and borrow from—the arts. Its purpose is selective, but its range is broad and varied.

This is advertising. This is publicity. This is public relations. It is television and radio, newspapers and magazines, direct mail and displays. This is a world of networks, printing and publishing, public relations counselors, advertising agencies and advertising departments, suppliers, media people, clients, repersentatives, marketing people, merchandising people. It is a world of commercial artists and commercial writers, photographers, designers, actors, salesmen, craftsmen—and pitchmen.

It is often a frantic world, always a fast-moving one. It can be everything or nothing, momentary or lasting, frustrating or satisfying.

All of you are a part of this world. You can't help but be. As consumers you are subject to some sixteen hundred advertising messages every day. Naturally you all have your own ideas about this force.

And, quite naturally, you have ideas about the people who create this force. You think of these people—and this work—as being honest or dishonest, helpful or harmful, masters of the art of falsehood or the compelling voice of the Great Age of Instant Hope, when all you have to do is add water. Anyway, think that 90 percent of the products you buy today were unknown ten years ago.

Many of us in communications—most of us, in fact—have an honest pride in our work. And we're honest too in admitting that we have problems. These are the problems we talked about to our minister, the problems we have hope of resolving by seeking guidance and direction through our Christian faith.

Honesty—an issue which everyone in every field shares, but one which is highlighted by the very nature of the communications field. "Truth in advertising" is no straw man the industry has set up to divert your attention. This is an actual practice, and an actual and ever-present problem.

It is a problem because we are sometimes called upon to promote the "structured truth," a truth that is based on what we can overlook or overemphasize. Some of us are called upon to promote products that are morally unacceptable or personally offensive. We may be called upon to justify what we do by the fact that somebody else in our field will do it if we don't. This is a fiercely competitive field. Accounts move fast and they move often, and so do the people who work in this field.

Honesty—that is an issue. So is integrity. We're in a business of personalities, a field where being "one of the boys" or being "yes men" can be regarded as a measure of our talent. Sometimes, for good or for bad, this is known as a "cooperative attitude."

What's more, in a business of ideas, as this is, we can't be "nine to fivers." We're never really finished with a job. We're charter members of the briefcase brigade. The demands of our work can take over completely and rob us of participation in constructive work in our communities, our schools, our church, or even with our own famiiles.

Communications is a creative business and calls for creative work. It is a field some of us have chosen because it is the one in which we can make the best total contribution—because it is rewarding, because it gives meaning and importance to our lives. We know this work can be done with dignity, pride, and joy. But we also know it can be the source of despair, disappointment, fear, grief—and many, many problems.

These, then, Dr. Kirkpatrick, are the issues that are ever present in the everyday work of communications—the issues and problems we seek help in resolving by turning to our Christian faith for discipline and direction.

SERMON: CHILDREN IN THE MARKET-PLACE

How can I describe the people of this generation? . . . They are like children sitting in the market-place and shouting at each other.—Luke 7:31-32

I

If you are in advertising and the minister says, "Bring your Bible and come to my office Thursday night—we'll seek help for your daily living," you'd do a couple of blinks inside where maybe he couldn't see.

The Bible? So we met, and I couldn't hold some of them back. They'd found all sorts of interesting and pertinent passages. Finally I got my chance to refer the group to one of my favorites, Habakkuk 2:2: "And the Lord answered me: 'Write the vision; make it plain upon tablets, so he may run who reads it.'" Obviously the birth of Burma-Shave ads.

At any rate, I'm grateful to these people and to all others who have opened my world a bit broader by sharing these discussions. Perhaps the usual demurrer should be entered right at the beginning—which goes something like this: "The opinions expressed are not to

25

be blamed on them, they are nobody's but my own!"

One can spend a lot of time in Proverbs noting the appropriateness of certain verses for advertising, primarily on the subject of honesty. Such as,

"Buy truth, and do not sell it." (23:23)

Or, "Lying lips are an abomination to the Lord, but those who act faithfully are his delight." (12:22)

Or, "Better is a little with righteousness than great revenues with injustice." (16:8)

Or, "The getting of treasures by a lying tongue is a fleeting vapor and a snare of death." (21:6)

But though proverbs are fun, it was when we come to Jesus' parable of the "peevish children" that we seemed to have found our real line.

"How can I describe the people of this generation? What are they like? They are like children sitting in the market-place and shouting at each other." (When I tried to write "market-place," as I reached for the "r" on my typewriter my fingernail hit the row of keys above and printed the $ instead—which perhaps is a slip with a meaning.)

What is the problem of the children who shout? Those who are shouted at don't respond appropriately.

"We pipe, we make music, we sing—and you won't dance."

"We weep, and wail—and you won't play funeral."

It's the complaint of the copywriter and all his colleagues in communication.

26

I spent a lot of time mulling over all that was said and written to me about the problems of this area of human endeavor and looking, as we who are in the business must do, for the key—the simple summation of the whole.

II

I've decided that the major moral question in communications is: *Who calls the tune?* Who calls the tune? —the customer, the competition, or the conscience?

The customer is a Big Man. He's got money. One of the ways of moving that money around is to make him want something he hasn't got, and then show him a slick picture of it. Put him in the picture and leave off mention of the price.

The New Testament piper didn't know what to do with his public—he piped but they wouldn't dance. Hal Wierwill would have offered a free course of twelve dance lessons followed by an inivitation to a presidential ball, and would not have failed to suggest that you could be the only one in your neighborhood to dance with Lady Bird! No point in giving up just because they don't respond—make them want to respond.

Some years ago I was on a committee of The Methodist Church planning research projects in preparation for programming a national urban-life conference. We decided that we needed a motivation study to determine why people choose to go to the church they do—or don't. I suggested we consult with large businesses to see how they determine buying motivation. So I asked a vice-president of one of the largest in the world. He said, "We don't try to discover what they want and then give it to them. We tell them what they want, and we've got it."

The customer—is he being treated like a human being by the trade?

Let it be said that my communications people and I are on good terms. I sensed immediately that they were pretty fed up with preachers who find it easy to tee off from the height of a pulpit on how the advertising game is the sole responsible agent in spoiling the morals and the values of the American public. They sensed almost as immediately, I think, that I wasn't going to indulge this fun sport but rather with them hoped we could find out how a Christian person faces the fact that he does have a powerful instrument in his hand when he has ideas and color pictures, a circulation of millions and purposeful writing.

One of the first obligations a Christian man has in the performance of his daily work is to accept honestly the amount of power he has over others. It is a fact no one can reasonably deny that advertising does shape values and develop attitudes. It is, and will continue to be, a factor in the shaping of our national character. There is much evidence that the advertising business accepts this, and with it accepts a certain responsibility. To read trade journals and house organs is to see editorials and articles which openly support certain moral and spiritual values in our common life and often take up the battle against certain evils: alcoholism, racism, isolationism, etc.

There is also always present the pressure to perform out of lesser motives, even to disregard this responsibility.

The individual who is a part of this vast complex but who wants to be truly a part of another world of commitment to Christian conduct will often find it a challenge to bring the two together.

The most determinative principle of all in this situation will be how he defines a man. The Christian faith offers us a Christian doctrine of man, which can't be fully stated here and now. The operational norm, however, which would result from looking at the customer from the standpoint of the Christian doctrine of man would be to treat him in the full integrity of his power to decide.

When we study how God deals with mankind, we are impressed by the true sense of freedom which he accords us. He, even he, never bulldozes over the integrity of man's power to make his choices.

The challenge offered by the Big Man and his money —the challenge to move his money around—seems fair sport. The greater challenge is to do it by appealing to the highest human motives and causing it to happen in the clean freedom of choice which is distinctively human.

Who calls the tune? The customer. But it's more complicated than that. There is also the competition (which

29

turns out to be the boss). If we go for business and someone else gets it, it is not their voice I hear, but the voice of the old man upstairs.

In one of the issues of *Advertising Age* is a report of one agency that pink-slipped thirty persons with a one-day notice. A major account shifted, and as one executive said, "We had a day to get out. Since it was a mass thing, we didn't want people standing around talking about it." Makes me feel real secure working for a bishop!

It certainly opens a new world to me. I don't have to read about it to know of it, however, for as I have visited my members in their offices, talked and prayed with them, I have realized what a precarious world it is— how swiftly and decisively one can get hurt, or see people he respects get hurt.

So it is not up to the preacher to form a moral code of conduct for a life he does not lead, but to honor those who do find, in the midst of shifting and threatening pressures, points of ultimate commitment which hold them steady.

But again I suggest that honest acceptance of the shape of the jungle one lives in is the surest way to keep from becoming a jungle man, or even aspiring to become Tarzan. Clients do feel they have a right to determine the image of what they want to show of their product; the agency may see this as false. The competition for sales puts pressure on to shape the presentation according to standards which may be personally offensive. There is always the problem of what to do about the "structured truth" and the "diagonal nod" (wonderful phrases—some of the rest of us will recognize that we find them useful too).

The answer to this one, it seems to me, lies in the direction of understanding the legitimate role of compromise. Or since "compromise" is a slippery word, I prefer to recommend that we all must determine the limits of our flexibility.

There are some things we don't like to do that we can do for the sake of a higher good. There are times when we can give assent, if only silent assent, to a condition of which we disapprove, but we must always know what we can do without sacrificing our integrity.

I discussed this with a young man who is in politics; having served many years in his state legislature, he is now in Congress. He has stood straight and strong for the Christian position on race in the midst of southern politics, and survived. He says there are any number of votes taken in the general assembly which are not morally crucial, and he can join people who disagree with him, but there are other times when he cannot. By doing the first he maintains his place even during the latter. This, he said, is a kind of compromise, but is Christian.

For years I was the pastor of a man who found himself in the lonely position of the top man in a great enterprise and thus was subjected to many powerful tensions. He was losing sleep and weight. I tried to get him to see that every man must go alone with himself and prayerfully draw a few lines beyond which he will never be pushed;

then he is free to operate with flexibility within the area this side of the line.

It's a bit strange, I guess, for the minister to be recommending compromise to ad men or to anyone in today's world. I am recommending flexibility, but more surely I am recommending clear-cut limits. Every man who knows where his limits are can be a happy operator. This is the New Testament meaning of the freedom of the committed man.

Who calls the tunes? The customer, the competition, or the conscience? Jesus said that John the Baptist had come acting one way, and the public didn't like him. Jesus came acting the opposite way, and the public complained about him too. So Jesus said we don't depend on what a modern writer has called the "other-directed" forces, but the "inner-directed" forces. "God's wisdom is proved right by all who are her children." (Luke 7:35.)

As the Christian faith calls on us and enables us to define and to treat other persons as truly human, so it calls on us and enables us to define and become true selves ourselves.

Here is a world frantic and fast moving, as Hal has said. There is the temptation to promise more than one can deliver, to let oneself, as a family man, a community man, and a churchman, be swallowed up by the pace. Here is a noisy world, and one is called on to create. The atmosphere needed for writing copy is the one the hymn writer described:

> Drop Thy still dews of quietness,
>   Till all our strivings cease;
> Take from our souls the strain and stress,
> And let our ordered lives confess
>   The beauty of Thy peace.

And it's a world of conventions and cocktail parties. Some of you think the preacher is the only person left who thinks social drinking is a moral question, but you just don't know how many times men and women from the world beyond these walls raise the question and seek a Christian answer.

All these and many more elements of life in the world of communications call on the Christian man to find his own personal identity somewhere else, so that when he comes into his world, he does not lose himself—as Alice forgot her name everytime she went into the woods, only to discover it again when she came out.

The Christian faith offers—as always—Christ. Here is a man who has no exterior contemporary marks on him, but is the true, essential, universal man. To know him is to know what every man is meant to be—and how to be it.

Dare I say it in the words of modern copy: "Down, cats, here comes the real Tiger."

III

This is not pulling him in at the last minute to make a bona fide sermon out of all this.

One of the most striking of all parallels between the communications industry and the Christian faith is the Christian concept of Christ as the Word. "The *Word* became flesh; he came to dwell among us, and we saw his glory." (John 1:14.)

What is a word in your trade? Somewhere is an idea —in some man's mind. That idea is to be transferred to another mind where it does not yet reside. How? A word does it. It is the bridge across which ideas move.

That's what Jesus Christ is. God's mind moves into ours—even ours—through the Word. If we learn to hear and identify that Word here in this place, we'll begin to recognize him over and over again in surprising places elsewhere, to our great benefit.

MEDICINE

CONVERSATION GUIDE

I. The Issues
   A. Motivations for medicine as a career.
   B. The doctor and the patient.
      1. Interpersonal relationships—factors of mobility, urbanization, specialization, etc.
      2. Difficulties of communication between patient and doctor.
      3. How can the religious commitments of the doctor serve the best interests of his patient? ("The physician can carry a great deal of the patient's load of anxiety on himself," a statement by one of the doctors in the group.)
      4. How to regard the patient as a person and not as a case.
      5. The role of prayer and faith in assuring the doctor that he is bringing his total best to the service of the patient.
      6. Should the patient be told the whole truth about his condition?
   C. The doctor as a person understanding himself and his vocation.

    1. Pressures toward fragmentation.

    2. External expectations—universities, government.

    3. Financial pressures leading to rationalizing a large number of visits for income purposes.

  D. Life versus death—the use of extraordinary measures to keep physical life going.

  E. Natural law versus civil law.

    1. Abortion—where the law allows a physician to do, for certain reasons, what is otherwise illegal. The decision regarding "certain reasons."

    2. Euthanasia—child hopeless at birth; the incurably ill aged.

    3. Sterilization.

  F. Institutional care versus home care.

    1. Children.

    2. Aged.

  G. Ministry to cases of a child born out of wedlock.

    1. Should the mother give up the child?

    2. How to deal with the father. (Conflict with philosophy of social workers.)

  H. The question of honesty.

    1. Causes of death on the death certificate. Autopsy.

    2. Drug prescriptions.

  I. The relation of illness to sin.

II. Beginning Thoughts

  A. The meaning of the paramount place of healing in Jesus' ministry.

    1. What does this say about the place of the body in Christian theology?

2. Has the church always been faithful to this con-concept of the body? Is this concept accepted or disputed by modern man?

3. Should the church emphasize Christian motivation (growing out of Jesus' healing ministries) in addition to other noble motivations in the recruitment of physicians from our young people?

4. Does the above fact say anything to the physician about his own self-understanding in relation to the pressures on him?

5. What is the relation of a Christian doctrine of creation to the healing ministry?

B. Methods the church can offer the doctor for personal strengthening.

C. The relation of body and soul.
1. Illness and guilt.
2. In what sense is healing a total act? Involving more than the physician? The lay ministry?

D. Should we raise the question of the financial image of the doctor and its relation to an image of conservatism?

III. Scripture to look at for direction
Matthew 4:23-25; 8–9; 10:1
Luke 7:18-23
John 9
I Corinthians 15:45-50.

STATEMENT OF THE ISSUES
by WILLIAM P. SWISHER, M.D.

It is with some awe and temerity that I speak for the medical profession, even with the able assistance of Doctors Latimer, Bailey, and Savage. One of the problems of this "corporate concern" is that no man can speak for such a large group. There must be room for a dissenting opinion. We are concerned that even the American Medical Association is so insecure that it does not publish an official dissenting opinion to the great controversial problems of the day.

I am also concerned about the effect on an already apprehensive public when doctors' fears, uncertainties, and concerns are made public.

Our concern begins with the patient-doctor relationship. We hold in our mind's eye the old family doctor who was always available, knew all the answers, and took over the responsibilities of getting the patient well. Today we live in a mobile, urban community where no one knows his patient for very long and perhaps has never seen him function in his family situation.

Twenty-five years ago the medical student was taught that the patient always had only one disease. Today, thanks to medicine, patients are living with several serious diseases and their complications. This is possible because of the marvelous teamwork of the hospitals, their laboratories, and a group of specialists. As seven or eight of these specialists parade through the patient's

38

room, who will stop to talk to and reassure the frightened patient? And if more than one person talks to him, will the stories be consistent?

An extremely important aspect of the patient-doctor relationship is communication between the two. The necessity to simplify the biological processes that are discussed is one source of misunderstanding. The fear and anxiety of the patient, who apprehensively picks up a hesitancy in speech or a qualifying word as evidence of information withheld, completely block the patient's acceptance of any explanation.

Should the patient be told of the seriousness of his illness? This is a question with a different answer every time it is presented. In general, a person who is mature enough to be responsible for himself or for others should be told. The way the situation is explained is as important as the information itself. A dogmatic statement should be avoided, since miracles do happen. The intelligent patient often asks the doctor if he has a certain disease before the doctor is able to answer. The physician must never remove hope from the patient's mind, since hope is a necessary ingredient for life.

The doctor in his profession is fragmented perhaps more than any other individual. In order to practice he may be required to give at least two half-days to teaching either at his hospital or his medical school or both. He must also give of himself for charity care. In trying to keep up his studying he is like Alice, who must run as fast as she can just to stay where she is. He should take

39

part in some research, and research introduces its own set of problems. He should be active in community affairs. If he neglects his family, by the time he is my age his life is an empty shell. He should be active in his church or synagogue. And, oh yes, incidentally, he must make a living for himself and his family.

The doctor also has personal problems. In following a patient he must decide how many visits are necessary to supervise the patient and support him through his illness, yet he must not step over that delicate border where the visit seems to have only an economic advantage for the doctor.

He must decide whether to prescribe a pill developed and made by American workers or one made more cheaply by foreign workers, its patents having been stolen. The problem of honesty in stating the cause of death on death certificates arises. He must use the terminology accepted by the state. As far as I know, no one has written "death from a broken heart," yet we all know of instances where this has occurred.

The doctor is concerned about the future of his profession and the scarcity of very high-quality students who are choosing medicine as a career. The great increase in need for service professions other than medicine has reduced the number of those interested in medicine as a service career. The prolonged period of training (from nine to eleven years beyond the four years for a bachelor's degree), which is also a period of dependency, is longer than that of any other profession and seems to

40

be an impossible length of time for many people. The newly trained doctor then enters a relatively short earning period which penalizes him from a taxation viewpoint. He also has no security for his family during these early years. Fortunately, youth in our culture have never yet backed down from a challenge.

Another area of concern for the doctor is the law. Many problems have not been worked out satisfactorily. We have a fairly good legal definition as to when life begins, although this is not without its controversial aspects. We do not know when life ends. This is particularly true today when newer techniques for organ replacements and the use of artificial respiration, artificial hearts, artificial kidneys, and artificial nutritional support prolong body metabolism long after the brain has deteriorated. One church attempts to solve this problem by stating that there are times when one need not use extraordinary means of sustaining life, but in our rapidly progressing time the extraordinary means of one year become the routine procedures of the following year.

Birth control information has legal obstacles in some states.

Abortion is allowed when it is performed for "certain reasons." These reasons depend on the judgment of a man. Often a patient will be refused an abortion in one hospital situation and be granted it immediately in another in the same area.

I need not mention the problems of euthanasia and

41

involuntary sterilization, since the law does not allow such procedures.

The doctor must be aware of the social implications of illness. Again he is part of a team with the hospital, the social worker, the family-welfare agency, and other community agencies. If the patient is a church member, the minister, priest, or rabbi can be very helpful in supporting the patient and his family through their emotional crisis. Some denominations are sending their young ministers to psychiatric training centers for special training in counseling.

Placing a child or an aged parent in a home or institution requires tact and skill to prevent the feeling of abandonment on the part of the placed person and to alleviate the guilt of the activating persons.

The care of the unmarried mother must include counseling with her parents to give them insight and understanding so that the family relationship can continue to be helpful and mutually supporting. The unwed father needs help with his feelings of guilt, inadequacy, and bewilderment. Here, too, the doctor, social worker, and minister must work together. In this cooperation the doctor must remember that it is the patient as a person that needs treatment and not the situation or disease. It is in his one-to-one relationship with the patient that the miracle of healing occurs.

SERMON: DR. JESUS
John 9

They asked him, "How were your eyes opened?" He replied,
"The man called Jesus made a paste."—John 9:11

I

Does the sermon title strike you as irreverent? Perhaps
tinged with blasphemy? Or just a suspicion of sensational
cheapness?

When the thought first came to me, I rejected it for all
these reasons, but then I reexamined the reasons. If I
had used the title, "The Great Physician," we wouldn't
have felt the same about it. It says the same thing. What's
the difference between calling him "the Great Physician"
and calling him "Dr. Jesus"? The first sounds more pious
—that's why I rejected it.

I didn't ask the doctors their opinion of such a title.
It only came to me later, but I would not have been
surprised to have them object. After all, there are too
many people running around using the title "Dr." who
are not trained in the medical profession. On certain air-
lines the stewardess asks if I'm an M.D.—just in case she
needs one. Usually she seems disappointed when I say,
"No, I'm a minister." Occasionally one with a sense of
humor may quip, "We may need you worse than an M.D."

Dr. Jesus—what right does he have to this title? He

couldn't pass medical examination boards, but the record of his case load is evidence of a busy practice.

However you interpret the record, one of the most obvious facts about Jesus' ministry is that he gave a very large place to the needs of the body. Passage after passage tells of individual healing or of a trip through villages and towns with multitudes of people benefiting from his touch or his word of compassion. In numerous places in the Gospels one runs across a passage like this one: "He went round the whole of Galilee, teaching in the synagogues, preaching the gospel of the Kingdom, and curing whatever illness or infirmity there was among the people. His fame reached the whole of Syria; and sufferers from every kind of illness, racked with pain, possessed by devils, epileptic, or paralysed, were all brought to him, and he cured them." (Matt. 4:23-24.)

This much is certain: the early church included in its description of Jesus' earthly ministry a very large concern for the physical needs of men. We have every right to believe that this attitude of the early church reflects an attitude Jesus himself held toward his mission on earth.

This clearly means that for the church in every century, including our own, healing is an essential, not a peripheral ministry. This is true not just because there are so many accounts of his healing miracles, but because the central doctrine of the Christian faith is the Incarnation. What higher dignity can be given to the human body than the doctrine which declares that God's supreme revelation of himself is through the clothing of divinity in flesh and blood? "The Word became flesh; and he came to dwell among us."

This is the foundation for a ministry of healing by the church, and it is the foundation whereby a physician can find a Christian understanding of the performance of his vocation.

No one would claim or believe that the extensive nature of the issues which confront a doctor who desires to make his profession a Christian witness could be dealt with in a few words. I have, however, chosen to address them on the basis of the incident recorded in the ninth chapter of John, for in a striking way so many of the issues we discussed in our sessions together were brought up in the conversations which took place concerning this account of the healing of the man blind from birth. Parenthetically, when preaching in the area of medicine and the Christian doctor, I am always tempted to use the scripture in Mark 5:25-26, where I smile every time I read, "And a certain woman, which had an issue of blood twelve years, And had suffered many things of many physicians, and had spent all that she had, and was nothing bettered, but rather grew worse" (KJV). But today we'll stay with the issues involved in the healing of the man blind from birth.

II

The one basic issue, it seems to me, for a Christian man who is a physician and who is trying to understand his

45

vocation in terms of his Christian commitments is how he answers this question: *"How were your eyes opened?"* Who opened this man's eyes? He said, "The man called Jesus made a paste. . . ." If a doctor is clear at this point, I believe he will find help in confronting many of the other issues in his practice.

One of these issues is brought up at the very opening of the account. His disciples put the question, "Who sinned, this man or his parents?"

Time and time again a doctor will find himself confronted by this question. It does no good for him to rule it out by saying that it is not strictly in his jurisdiction to deal with it. His patients will continue to ask it, and it will continue to ask itself deep inside him. "Why was he born blind?"

The question "Is there a relation of sin to body distress?" still plagues us. Job didn't settle it. Every man must ask it again for himself.

The answer is yes and no. No, in the sense that God is not arbitrarily dropping punishment on us in the form of cancer or broken legs because we sin. Yes, in the sense that disease of the spirit, which is what sin is, disturbs the wholeness of the personality. Thus, when we are guilty of sin, we are not well—this may or may not show up in bodily symptoms. Wholeness is God's will for us, and that wholeness is not possible if there is physical or spiritual disease. So God's will is always healing.

In answer to the disciples' question about the blind man, Jesus said two things. He said quite clearly that neither this man nor his parents had sinned. But he "was born blind *that* God's power might be displayed in curing him." This is not meant to say that God sports with us—making babies blind so he can show off later. No, not that. But, rather, that every need of man, body and soul, must be seen to be an opportunity, an occasion, for the operation of God's power in man's life.

It's something like this: on a lovely spring day a field is covered with fresh spring flowers. A farmer plows his field, tearing it apart. He makes holes in the ground every few inches for the length of the field. A passerby says, "What a shame—a field of naked holes." "But no," says the farmer, "into each hole I drop a seed; the holes are there as places where new life can come forth and food be produced."

Every Christian man is to look out on his world with its vast need and agony not to bemoan it, but gratefully and joyfully to see it all as opportunity for the power of God to be revealed.

The second thing he said in answer to this question was: "While daylight lasts we must carry on the work of him who sent me." That is to say, every occasion of need is a call to us to join God in the work of applying his power to the curing of the need.

The doctors express two concerns which, I think, are addressed by this kind of understanding of need. They talk about the motivations which are needed by young men and women if they are to choose medicine as a career and commit themselves to the disciplines of training. They also talk, as almost everybody does these days, of the pressures which tend to fragment them personally.

Is not the answer to both these contained in a deep insight into these statements of our Lord? A body not whole offers itself as an opportunity for God's power to be revealed in the world. It also offers a call to men to join in the activity of revealing God's power. This opportunity and duty call many to enter medicine and offer the maturing man an inner discipline and a single center to hold him together against the fragmenting pulls.

A second and very real concern of physicians is the doctor-patient relationship.

Our society is impersonalizing so many of our relationships. A sensitive doctor sees the danger of this happening to his relationship with his patients. There are difficulties in communicating because the doctor lives in and knows well a world which is strange to the patient, a world into which he has suddenly and unwillingly been plunged. How can the doctor's own religious faith carry some of the weight that belongs to the patient? What role do prayer and faith on the part of the doctor have in assuring that he is bringing his best to the service of the patient? Should the patient be told the whole truth about his own condition?

I have repeated these questions because there is great significance in the fact that they are asked by doctors. The kind of doctor who is asking these questions is a doctor who has not lost the sensitivity necessary for a good personal relationship with the patient. There isn't much that is specific in the incident of Jesus and the man blind from birth which will serve as a guidepost, but just to read and reread this chapter is to begin to get a feeling of the kind of relationship which is evident between this man and Jesus. To feel it is to begin to possess it. Verses 6 and 7 record how Jesus made the paste and put it on the man's eyes and then ordered him to go to the pool of Siloam and wash, which he did. Here are two people working together in a kind of harmony, even unity, and it took them both to accomplish the final healing.

If any one of us wants to become the kind of person who has the best possible relationships with other people, there is no guidebook of little rules, but there is a person who comes so vividly alive in the New Testament that to know him well is to become like him in dealing with others.

In the third place there are a number of hard choices which a doctor must make. These men tell me they can be defined under the larger question of natural law versus civil law.

For example, the civil law makes abortion illegal, yet there are occasions when it seems right to the physician to perform an abortion. The law may even allow him, for certain reasons, the discretion to perform what otherwise would be illegal. Here is an area where the physician is alone with his conscience. There are numerous other examples, of course—euthanasia, sterilization, listing causes of death on the death certificate, reporting the results of autopsies, handling drug prescriptions. The dilemmas broaden further to include decisions about institutional care versus home care and dealing with unwed mothers and fathers and their children.

What is the law by which the physician determines his choices—civil law, custom, church law, natural law —or is there an ultimate will of God? If there is, can he find it? If he finds it, dare he believe that it would be practical in his daily world? If so, what right has he to choose to obey the highest law, if others, affected by his choice, do not recognize the same understanding of God's law that he does?

No preacher would be presumptuous enough to offer himself as the answer box out of which come solutions to such excruciating dilemmas.

We do well, however, to note that we have the opportunity to see Jesus caught in exactly the same squeeze. The Pharisees raised the question. It was a sabbath day. Now don't lose touch with the truth that is here just because we don't hold to the same interpretation of the sabbath that the Pharisees did. Neither did Jesus; that is the exact point of his helpfulness to us. There has always been a strong weight of opinion which says, "This fellow is no man of God; he does not keep the law," or "We know that God spoke to Moses, but as for this fellow, we do not know where he comes from" (John 9:16, 29). Here is the whole dilemma between law, custom, and tradition and an individual action based on conscience. Jesus gives no clear-cut answer here except to

50

say that the Pharisees think they see but are really blind. We all know he was saying that there is a final, ultimate voice which speaks to a man, and the man must obey it. Such a man will not always be rewarded by the applause of the community, but if that is what he wants, he must sometimes forfeit the inner satisfaction of knowing the pleasure of God on his choices.

What can the Christian gospel offer a man who must find strength inside himself for such hours? We offer him the Christian church, which must ever strive to be a fellowship where men are valued because they seek to choose the right as God reveals it to them. A fellowship which meets together regularly for mutual instruction, for the empowering of the inner life which comes from prayer and all other acts of worship. A fellowship which by its continuity represents stability over the long pull of the truth. To be a part of such a group of people means that difficult days do not become defeating days.

We come back again, finally, to the first and basic question: What happened here? How was this man healed? Who healed him?

Throughout its history Nepal has refused admission to Christian missionaries. A few years ago, however, the king invited a united medical mission to establish work. Now there is an impressive string of projects throughout that mountain kingdom. Dr. Edgar Miller of the staff of the hospital in Kathmandu was kind enough to take me to visit the Chini Lama, the head of the Buddhists in Nepal. The Chini Lama had a cousin who was in the

Christian hospital. She had been brought in unconscious and remained so for several days; however, she had responded well. Now, reported Dr. Miller, she was well enough to be dismissed, but she resisted leaving the hospital because she enjoyed it so there. The Lama called to a servant to bring a Buddhist calendar, and then he proceeded to show us some signs and symbols, trying to explain their meaning. He said to Dr. Miller, "I told her many months ago that the signs in our calendar showed that she would have a major illness. I advised her to buy many extra prayer flags that she might not die." As we drove away in the mission jeep, I said to Dr. Miller, "It raises an interesting question in theology. You think it was our Christian medicine that healed her. The Chini Lama thinks his prayer flags and calendar did it!"

So, too, that day when Jesus healed the blindman. There were many different opinions, as there are yet. The Jews would not believe that the man had been blind. There is always the attitude that the evil or the disease didn't really exist, so nothing happened. We can, if we choose, deny the facts. The parents knew the facts but had no faith interpretation of what had happened. They were afraid of the Jews. In our culture, too, there are always people who never get to the truth of God's actions in the lives of men, because they are afraid to admit to their neighbors that they see what the neighbors do not see.

The man himself came down hard on the side of the factuality of the faith. He knew what had happened, and he was open to any explanation of who made it happen.

Jesus stands in the middle of these various opinions as the stone of stumbling. The whole of what we believe happened here depends on what we believe about Jesus. If we believe one thing about him, then it is no strain to accept a dramatic miracle, a unique, supernatural intervention. If we believe something else about Jesus, this is not acceptable and so the whole interpretation of the passage is changed.

III

That, of course, is the essential dividing question—the nature of Jesus Christ. As the title itself raised questions about him, so the whole problem of human existence is in deciding what we believe about him.

"A man called Jesus made a paste. . . ."

To the Christian church through the centuries this has meant that God is interested in the wholeness of every person. It means that in some special sense we know this about God because we learn it from the healing ministry of Jesus. And, therefore, if we are Christian people —that is to say, people whose central loyalty is shaped by our relationship to Jesus Christ—then we are *all* called to a ministry of healing in his name.

Certain ones among us will feel themselves called

into the discipline of medicine. It is the ministry of the church to seek to assist such ones among us in finding ways to shape their practice of their vocation so as to express the finest and best that we learn from Christ about God and his desires for his people.

LAW

CONVERSATION GUIDE

I. The Issues

  A. Whether law and morality are the same.

    1. The issues that come up in ordinary practice are not clear-cut moral issues. The right is obscure, ambiguous, or shared, so that the lawyer must go to a technical point for the settlement. Both sides have some right on their side, so a basis other than right must be found for the settlement.

    2. "The safest way to make laws respected is to make them respectable. When law and morality contradict each other, the citizen has the cruel alternative of either losing his moral sense or losing his respect for the law. These two evils are of equal consequence." [1]

    3. In the Evanston Conference of Lawyers and Clergymen this issue was introduced by the following statement in a letter from a lawyer to a clergymen: "The first thing that I am curious about is: What is the understanding of law that

[1] Frederic Bastiat, *The Law*, trans. Dean Russell (Irvington-on-Hudson, N. Y.: Foundation for Economic Education, 1950), p. 12.

we are dealing with? Law, basically, is a working agreement between members of a community, the violation of which will be punished either by force of one form or another or financial penalty of one form or another. This agreement between the members of the community is generally considered a compact that is necessary for civilized living." What happens to the concepts of natural law and divine law under this definition?

B. Whether justice is done when the service of lawyers is more available to some segments of the population than others. What is a lawyer's obligation to justice in a case when he is aware of possessing superior strength over his antagonist—a superior strength resulting from an imbalance of knowledge or some other factor not strictly related to justice?

C. What is the Christian attitude toward litigation?

  1. Most lawyers spend most of their time counseling and arranging peaceful settlements of affairs. Litigation is necessary, however, to supply a common law for society. Lawyers have a most effective place and opportunity in dealing with people to serve as lay ministers. Lincoln: "As a peacemaker a lawyer has a superior opportunity of being a good man."

  2. The value in the slowness of legal processes.

II. Beginning Thoughts

  A. Are these all the really pertinent issues in your life as a Christian and your practice of law?

B. The legal tradition has been to acknowledge the right of a man to be regarded innocent until proved guilty and to be faced by his accusers. Are there factors in American life which work toward changing this tradition? What are they? Should they be allowed to continue? What can the lawyer do at this point? What can the ordinary citizen do?

C. Ought we not recognize that there may be differences between man's law and divine law and that a man with Christian commitments to the ultimacy of the latter may have decisions to make which fall back finally on individual conscience?

D. Ought we not recognize that the Christian faith conceives of a fellowship society which would differ in significant ways from an ordinary pluralistic society of organized law, and that the Christian man will always find himself living in the two at the same time?

III. Scripture to look at for direction

Matthew 5:38-45

Luke 10:25-37

Romans 13:1-6

I Corinthians 6:1-8

The whole concept of law versus grace

Matthew 5:17-18

Romans 7:6

Galatians 3:24

Hebrews 10:1

What is the modern counterpart to this use of law?

Lawyers: Luke 10:25; 11:46; 14:3; Titus 3:13
Lawgivers
  Exodus 34:32
  Deuteronomy 4:44; 33:4
  Isaiah 33:22; 51:4
  John 1:17; 7:19
  Acts 7:35-38
  James 4:12

STATEMENT OF THE ISSUES
by JOHN D. HASTINGS

Dr. Kirkpatrick asked us: "What are the special situations in the practice of law to which we want our Christian faith to speak?"

We answered that in the day-to-day practice of law Christian principles as such do not provide relevant guides for handling or solving the problems with which a lawyer works. Is it the blindness of the specialist that leads us to say that the problems in the practice of law can be and are solved by the technicalities and craftsmanship of the law? Like a carpenter cutting a true line or a bridge builder applying sound mathematics, we find that the techniques of our craft are more useful than the Sermon on the Mount. In almost all cases, right, justice, and fairness are pretty evenly divided between the parties.

None of us could recall a situation in which performing our duty to a client involved disregarding Christian

58

teaching, except possibly divorce proceedings. Even there, what is the meaning of Jesus' teaching on divorce for the lawyer as well as the husband and wife? We lawyers do not, of course, advise a man who has lost his house by foreclosure to turn over his car or give his shirt to the mortgage lender. If Jesus' techings require otherwise, then we are clearly violating them. Does Jesus assert that the principles in the Sermon on the Mount should be embodied in the law of the land?

When a man has obeyed the law, has he done all that Christianity calls upon him to do? Or has he laid the groundwork from which he can go forward to the area with which Jesus was concerned—the area beyond the law? Is mere compliance with the law—even with all the 613 commandments of the Hebrew religious and civil law—enough? What relation is there between Jesus' teaching of inner righteousness and public regulations?

In the year 1900 lawyers could not say what we have said. Almost all the major fields of the law have changed greatly in two generations and have come much closer to reflecting Christian standards. Have the teachings of the church influenced the legislation and attitudes which produced these changes? Can the social gospel of Washington Gladden, Walter Rauschenbusch, William Temple, Harry Emerson Fosdick, Harris Franklin Rall, and Ernest Fremont Tittle, working through dedicated laymen and lawyers, be given a good share of the credit for ameliorating the harshness of the old law?

More important—is there work still to be done? Can

church members inspire and guide us toward better laws and a better legal order? What legal help does our submerged fifth need? How can it be provided? Are there bills now on the docket which we as lawyers and you as laymen should support or oppose because of their compatibility or incompatibility with our Christian faith? What guidance does that faith give us in applying the modern concepts of rehabilitation to our inadequate workman's compensation law or to the slaughter and mayhem that go on hour by hour on our highways?

These are all prosaic and workaday problems in a sense, but can we not say with George Herbert:

> Who sweeps a room, as for Thy laws,
> Makes that and the action fine.

SERMON: SUE FOR YOUR SHIRT
Deuteronomy 1:13-18; 16:18-20

If a man wants to sue you for your shirt, let him have your coat as well.—Matthew 5:40

I

Sir Edward Coke in the sixteenth century gave rules for the use of the hours of the day by lawyers: six hours of sleep, six hours in law, two hours at meals, four hours at prayer, and "what is over bestow upon the Sacred Muses." In our discussions, I found no one who confessed to spending four hours a day at prayer!

Reginald Hine in his *Confessions of an Un-common Attorney* is the one who cites this antiquated advice. He goes on to characterize those who are with him in the legal profession:

By common repute we lawyers are an irreligious race. Once, indeed, I heard a client declare that we deserved to be "exiled from the eternal providence." And the reasons are manifest. In the first place our spiritual and moral sensibilities are apt to grow blunt under the wear and tear of daily practice. Day in and day out—making the worst appear the better reason—we are defending men and women who have been breaking every letter of the Decalogue. . . .

Then, too, we are by our training circumspect and critical. We expect proof positive in matters of faith where no such proof can be. . . . It is of no avail to cite Pascal's *obiter dictum:* "The heart has its reasons which Reason knows not," for if we possessed a heart, which is commonly denied, we would not allow it to sway our judgment or supplant the laws of evidence. . . . Like doubting Thomas we refuse to believe unless we see. . . .

We go home burdened and bewildered with the problems of the day, and there are papers in our portfolio for the morrow. "I am generally so dead beat by the time I kneel down to pray," said Henry Hawkins, "that I begin out of habit: 'Gentlemen of the jury.' " [2]

I personally am happy to come to the defense of the lawyers, if the defenders need a defender. Many times I have known great lawyers who are great Christians.

[2] (New York: The Macmillan Company, 1947), pp. 245-46.

Our lawyers do say, however, that they need a defender. The first thing they want me to make clear to the rest of you is that all lawyers are not like all other lawyers. The vocation is so broad that it includes criminal lawyers, personal-injury lawyers, divorce lawyers ("these are important," said one of our members, "but are a very small percentage of the legal profession, and are little more representative of all than Billy Graham is of all the ministry"), tax lawyers, patent lawyers, antitrust lawyers, labor lawyers, members of corporate legal departments, international lawyers, law teachers, etc. Not only are the persons involved different from one another, but the issues will differ from one field to the next.

As a matter of fact, it has interested me to see how concerned each profession is about its public image. Lawyers don't want to be thought of as Perry Masons; doctors, as Dr. Kildares; and public relations men, as Madison Avenue.

But whether or not lawyers are thought of as any more or less religious than others, the concept of—indeed the word—law fills scripture. To read anywhere in the Old or New Testaments is to come upon a discussion of law. The longest chapter in the Bible—Psalms 119—has law as its single theme and has sometimes been known as the lawyers' psalm.

The conversations I had with these men were in striking contrast to most of the other conversations. There was almost no talk of various specific issues which face these men in a day's work. One of my conceptions of a lawyer—perhaps a misconception—has been that of a person who centers on the picayune detail, one who works with the specific, the very specific. But this was not the case in our discussions. Most of the time was taken in abstract definitions of law and its place in society.

So that the question for today is inevitably posed: What is the law? What does the Christian faith teach us is the law?

II

A lawyer is a person who handles the law. *What is the law?* A Christian lawyer will want to know the Christian understanding of the law he handles.

There is a dinner group known as the Evanston Conference of Lawyers and Clergymen. After one of the sessions a lawyer wrote to the minister who had chaired the meeting: "It would appear that one of our first orders of business would be to reach some kind of conclusion or definition of what we mean by the word 'law.'"

In the meeting that followed the writing of this letter it was quite obvious that, though our group was small, we would never come to an agreement on a basic definition of law.

The writer of the letter had said that law "is a working agreement between members of a community, . . . a compact that is necessary for civilized living." Is that the way you would define law?

The Old Testament idea is not that of a group of

people who decide to live together and agree on certain laws for the sake of living together peaceably. Rather it pictures a group of people called into being by God led by a charismatic leader selected by God. This leader—Moses—was directed to go to the top of a mountain where amidst the pagaentry of fire, cloud, and deep gloom a loud voice spoke the basic law. Then God —with some kind of Cecil B. DeMille finger—wrote the law on two stone tablets for a permanent record.

So here are two extremes—one says law is nothing but a mutual agreement among people, and the other says law is a solemn command written in stone by the hand of God.

The second interpretation applied to a community which is made up of a single race will produce what we have in the Old Testament—the history of a nation in which civil law and religious law are one and the same, with the result that almost without exception when the word "law" is used by Jesus or Paul, it refers to this combination of civil and religious law. New Testament lawyers were on the staff of the temple.

This is not the kind of community in which we live. Ours is pluralistic and complex in a number of other ways. Consequently, we are confronted by many different levels of law—perhaps even different kinds of law. How we handle the law, either as lawyers or citizens, depends on how we understand and define these various levels.

There are laws that are nothing more than living arrangements with other people. When I run a red light,

I have violated such an arrangement. Whether I have done anything more than that or not depends on other ethical and religious presuppositions which I as an individual have accepted.

When a citizen murders another citizen, he has seriously violated the living arrangement. Maybe he has done more. Society has, up to now, generally believed it had the right to punish him by killing him in turn. Whether the citizen did anything more than violate a human arrangement again depends on the larger religious context a person or a society acknowledges.

The debate which, fortunately, is growing in our time over the question of whether or not society has the right or whether it ought to take his life will find persons on the same side of the debate holding their same viewpoint out of very different interpretations of law and right. Some will object to capital punishment on pure human bases—it isn't effective; it is primitive; etc. Others will likewise oppose capital punishment on the grounds that it violates divine law.

These are illustrations—and anyone can multiply them —where in our lives we are caught having to give differing degrees of obedience to laws depending upon the differing degrees of authority attributed to the many kinds of laws in our lives.

This, quite obviously, is no more a problem for the professional lawyer than for any of us. What is the law? is a daily question every man must answer.

A scriptural understanding of life and law, I submit, includes the following basic principles:

There is a fundamental orderliness in the cosmos and in meaningful human life which can be discerned and codified, though always with a respectful tentativeness.

Men of religious faith have in all centuries attributed this order to God, and have believed that the ways of men are meant to conform to the will of God.

Therefore, the *highest* law, the *supreme* authority, for the committed man is the law of God.

He endeavors to live by it, and to bring the society of which he is a citizen under the judgment of God to reform it in accordance with God's law. (One lawyer in our group strongly expressed his opinion that lawyers should have given more leadership in changing the civil rights conditions of this nation. Others said they had; others said they shouldn't.)

He recognizes that he must always test his individual understanding of God's law by reference to the understanding of the larger community, which is the church.

He knows himself to be living in the rare gift of freedom which God gives to all who are obedient to his will.

He acknowledges that there is a way of life "beyond the law" to which he will be led if he gives himself to a life of love.

These basic understandings of life and law, then, shoot out in all directions with multiple implications.

At the most elemental level the Christian lawyer will conduct himself according to the highest precepts of his profession, knowing that by so doing he is contributing to the orderliness and well-being of himself and his fellows. It may be that there is no difference here between the man of active faith and the lawyer of no faith, if both are men of professional integrity.

But the lawyer who is a Christian man of real faith will find dimensions opening to him in his personal living and in his professional practice which are considerably beyond this elemental integrity.

"If a man wants to sue you for your shirt," Jesus said, "let him have your coat as well." What kind of advice is that for lawyers? This is not a recommendation against litigation in the body politic. Neither is it the fancy of an impractical, desert-dwelling religious recluse. It is a way of life which some men, out of special motivations, do adopt. It is the attitude of a man who, being compelled by the law to go a mile, out of love chooses to go two miles.

It is not a rule that will work in our kind of society. Nor is it a rule that must wait for the emergence of the perfect society. It is a way of life some men choose even in our present kind of society.

Law and religion both speak to the same stubborn fact: in man there is a natural unwillingness to consider other men's interests equal to his own.

Because this is true, lawyers find themselves with considerable work to do—and good incomes! What theologians have labeled original sin is the natural self-centeredness of the human being, a self-centeredness that clashes with the self-centeredness of other individuals. This calls for someone to serve as arbitrator. This is one way to deal with the problems of human relationships— a civilized way.

There is another way—a better way. It is the way of Christ. The law of love. It results from one man's willingness to consider the interests of other men equal to or even above his own. What motivates a man to adopt such an attitude toward others? Love. The loving family is an ideal illustration of such a relationship. The church, when it is true to itself, is an even better example because in the true church this law of love operates even apart from blood-tie responsibilities.

"Love," wrote Paul, "is the fulfilling of the law" (Rom. 13:10 RSV).

III

It's not an easy way of life. There is a sense in which it is easier to be a law-abiding citizen than to be a person who lives up to the law of love.

The man who lives by the law of love does live in considerably more freedom than other men; in fact, there are some who believe this is the only true freedom there is—this freedom in Christ. But though he lives in freedom beyond the law, he will not be without conflicts. If someone slaps him on one cheek and he offers the other, he will probably get slapped on that one too!

The point is that law is necessary in a society of natural men, but there is a life better than that produced by the law. It is the life of love. As Martin Luther King said in this pulpit, "The law can't make you love me, but it can keep you from lynching me." Christ, not the law, makes it possible for us to love one another.

If a lawyer, therefore, is faithful to his profession, he does a good thing for his society. If a lawyer is a man in Christ, he will be living according to a superior set of principles which will often place him in tension with his society, even at its best. But it will be a creative tension out of which comes a new kind of justice.

All of us are called to be Christian citizens. This means being obedient to the laws of men, but for a reason higher than self-interest. It means, however, being always obedient to the laws of God. If we are caught in a conflict between the laws of men and the laws of God, we have no doubt where our supreme authority is found. If you dislike calling this civil disobedience, then call it what it truly is—divine obedience, a loyalty we must never surrender.

Being Christian citizens, we will hold the interests of others in the same light in which God through Christ holds us—with the result that through acts of loving obedience to the highest ordinances there will emerge a new type of justice and a new life of freedom. Let us pray, using Samuel Johnson's prayer for those who study law:

Almighty God, the Giver of wisdom, without Whose help resolutions are vain, without Whose blessing study is ineffectual, enable us, if it be Thy will, to attain such knowledge as may qualify us to direct the doubtful, and terminate contentions. And grant that we may use that knowledge which we shall attain, to Thy glory and our own salvation; for the sake of Jesus Christ our Lord. Amen.

BUSINESS

CONVERSATION GUIDE

I. The Issues

    A. Is the Christian ethic different from any normal ethic, or is this an out-dated idea? Is there a Protestant ethic? If a business association has a code of ethics, is this sufficient, or does a personal ethic go beyond a group statement?

        1. TV claims there are no problems in network television that are not shared by all other businesses whose primary responsibility is communication with the public. Are there no unique moral issues, then, that belong to this business? Is it true that television is simply a whipping boy and is not capable of being good or bad?

        2. If responsibility can be passed on to others by this group, can't everyone blame someone else? Salesmen can blame management; management can blame the public.

        3. "Good business is synonymous with the Christian ethic." True or false?

        4. Honesty and integrity in the sales of municipal bonds. Is it just good business or ethics?

        5. One member insisted there is fantastic honesty in

business—if one is caught once in a dishonesty, he has destroyed his future.

B. Labor-management relations.

1. Satisfaction with mediocrity. Is this a symptom of our times?

2. How to recover the individual's sense of responsibility to perform daily duties with a pride of accomplishment.

3. How to motivate an individual to work with independent initiative, yet be an enthusiastic part of the total organization.

4. Labor and management negotiations—marked by responsibility for Christian leadership, responsibility for mutual understanding of each party's position, and concern to avoid moral, economic, and physical hardships. "Right to work" versus closed shop.

5. Fair employment practices. What responsibility does a businessman have to do what is "right" if it has no economic relationship to the business, or may even result in a penalty?

6. Responsibility in the face of automation.

C. Obligation of management to stockholders.

D. Responsibility of international business for goodwill toward our country and its ideals. Responsibility of international business for bringing pressure against evil in other governments, such as those of South Africa, Rhodesia, Portugal, Russia, China.

E. Companies and charitable giving.

F. Pressures on the individual to break his personal commitments regarding liquor, sex, etc.

G. Hypocritical approach of giving lip service in church yet holding a different attitude during the week.

II. Beginning Thoughts

    A. In what sense does the modern world make Christian ethics based on the New Testament out of date?

        1. Many modern dilemmas are not faced in scripture because they were not a part of the New Testament world.

        2. Where, then, does a modern man get guidance from his religion, or is religion irrelevant?

    B. Is there any sense in which we can regard our work as a part of a larger plan of God's intention to accomplish something permanent for mankind?

    C. Doesn't it follow that we need help in deciding what we can control in our lives and what to do about the areas of which we are not in control? Would such a decision give a man a sense of security?

    D. Will a Christian view of man save us from the usual pitfall of regarding people as groups?

III. Scripture to look at for direction

    Proverbs 10:4; 11:1; 21:6; 22:29

    Matthew 6:24; 22:1-10

    Luke 12:16-21; 16:13

    Romans 12:11, 17

STATEMENT OF THE ISSUES
by DWIGHT L. MYERS

I represent the businessmen's group; we were selected by Dr. Kirkpatrick to represent activity in various types of businesses.

In our first meeting each member described some existing and growing problem and how it is related to the present-day business world. These problems were thoroughly discussed from the standpoint of arriving at some possible solution which could come from a well-grounded Christian faith.

At a later meeting Dr. Kirkpatrick asked us all to bring our Bibles, and we again embarked upon the task of interpreting these problems, using both the precepts of a Christian faith and the interpretation of the written word from the Scriptures.

It is an accepted fact that the strongest precept in sound business management is honesty of performance. Even with this as an accepted fact, we did introduce into the discussions many things that would indicate that in the past twenty years there has been a moral decay and a marked compromise of morals in general, as well as of principles and ethics. Some of us also felt that in these topsy-turvy times a contributing cause is the fact that people just don't care enough about each other—as they once did.

An interesting discussion centered around the matter of mediocrity in business today and how it has crept into the employed person's attitude toward his job. Cheating on the time allowances for coffee breaks is an example of this attitude as is the growing satisfaction of many people with doing their job just well enough to get by, rather than doing it as well as they know how.

Labor and management relations were considered. Specifically, we discussed the "right-to-work" theory versus the closed shop. Fair employment practices on the part of employers and managements' responsibilities to their stockholders were both seen as part of these problems.

Using the Bible as our reference and guide, we faced the fact that modern dilemmas are not easily identified in the Scriptures because they were not a part of the New Testament world. This poses a question: Where, then, does a man go today for his guidance in order to establish for himself a sound Christian approach to his everyday business life?

One of the most stimulating sessions was focused on the matter of labor-management relations. The greatest success in such matters always comes when there is a mutually honest approach on both sides. Negotiations such as these accomplish beneficial results more quickly and soundly and often avoid moral, economic, and, at times, physical hardships.

This has been a most rewarding and educational experience for all of us. We are hopeful that each of you will gain the same stimulation and satisfaction we did in this most inspiring experience.

SERMON: MAMMON IS MY BOSS
Luke 12:13-21

You cannot serve God and Money.—Matthew 6:24

I

The same conditions in eighteenth-century England which produced Wesley's evangelical revival also produced Marxism.

John Wesley preached to the miners and instituted, in the name of God, social reforms that are credited with saving England from a French Revolution. Karl Marx holed himself up in the British Museum and reacted to the capitalism of his day by writing *Das Capital,* the bible of communism.

This is proof enough that there is more than one way to look at the same set of economic facts.

It was near the end of our evening of Bible study when I pointed out to our group of businessmen the passage in Matthew where Jesus said, "You cannot serve God and mammon." Only some of us had the New English Bible, which puts it all in words we understand, "You cannot serve God and Money." That produced a reaction! For, they reminded me, they are men who work for money. Does Jesus mean you must choose between working for God and working for money?

The crux of the whole matter in a Christian interpretation of the business life is the question of whether working for God and working for money are one and the

76

same thing; whether they are two separate things yet compatible; or whether they are two separate things and incompatible.

Kierkegaard points out that Jesus didn't say you must not or you should not serve God and mammon. He said you *cannot.*

In *The Mansion* William Faulkner describes the funeral of Flem Snopes. It was a big funeral. He was a prominent banker and financier, but he had died and was being buried under no auspices: neither fraternal, civic, nor military—only finance. He belonged "simply to Money. He had been a member of a Jefferson church, true enough, . . . but even that had been not a subservience nor even an aspiration nor even really a confederation nor even an amnesty, but simply an armistice temporary between two irreconcilable tongues."

"Two irreconcilable tongues"—"you cannot serve God and Money."

II

This all serves to get us quickly into the primary question: *Is there a Christian ethic which is different from any ordinary ethic?*

In the discussion groups of each profession there was expressed in some way or other the question of whether the Christian standard is something other than the ordinary good ethical life. "Good business," said one man, "is synonymous with the Christian ethic." "Honesty is the best policy" is an old adage. Every business association and professional group has its code of ethics. If a person adheres to this code, isn't that sufficient? Wouldn't that make him a pretty good Christian? No.

It is true that the standards of the American business community show many evidences of the molding effects of the Christian conscience. We are hearing an abundance of criticism of the church for being irrelevant. We are, on the other hand, confronted by a mounting attitude which criticizes the church for placing itself openly against the evils of our day. Let it be recognized that the preaching of the prophets of the social gospel in the past fifty years has had a tremendous effect on reshaping the conscience of the American business community. And when people nostalgically declare that Grandfather's days were more religious days, don't you believe it. That kind of statement can only be made out of naïveté, not out of any kind of knowledge of our history. John Hastings, in his statement of the issues involved in law, called off the names of men who represent a whole movement of the past generation in which the church of this country led this nation nearer to a true ethical base in its social, economic, and political life. There is yet more of this kind of leadership necessary for the church to give in our time.

It is the success of the church at this point that creates the problem we now have of seeing the radical separation still and always existing between the ethic of our culture and the Christian ethic.

The improvement of certain ethical standards through social legislation and through business, professional, and labor standards of ethics is to be appreciated. Further improvement is always to be sought.

However, the Christian ethic will always remain something other than the cultural ethic. This difference is not to be judged by degrees. That is to say, we don't simply say that a Christian man is, or is expected to be, more honest than a businessman who makes no claim to religious faith.

The Christian ethic grows out of the decision about one's ultimate loyalty.

When Jesus said a man can't serve God and money, he did so in the context of a discussion about slavery. A slave, he said, can't be owned by two owners. No one will quarrel with that statement.

In the same sense we cannot have two ultimates in our lives. When we push to the topmost level of our lives, there is a single command post—the question for all of life is: Who occupies the command post?

In the complex structure of our lives there are many levels of command, just as there are many levels of commands in any military organization. There is a sense in which we take orders from, we work for, the many lower commands, but we must do so only in agreement with the ultimate authority.

The Christian ethic is a straight line from where I am daily to God's will for me. Money is not bad, neither is it good. If it is on the line, it is good; if it is not, it is evil.

There is only one voice that can speak the ultimate word of command in our lives. One of the most instructive and redemptive things a man can do is be honest enough with himself to probe to see whose voice it is that speaks the final word of authority.

It can't be both God and money. It can't be both God and anything else.

When a man knows whose voice speaks the final word of authority in his own life, then he has all he needs for direction in the decisions he must face in business or anywhere else.

Such a man is not honest because his business association has sent him a plaque for his office wall which says everybody in this business is honest.

Such a man is not honest because it is good business. He's honest when it isn't good business.

The scale of values which such a man applies to his life and his business is the scale of values which is consistent with the desire of the one who is his ultimate boss.

Jesus told an interesting parable about the man whose business was good—very good. The Dow-Jones averages in his life were way high. He made a lot; he had to expand. Jesus didn't say there was anything wrong with that, as such. He just reminded the man that values are determined by the total picture, and the total picture includes the ultimate questions: When you're dead, who

80

gets your money? And when your money's taken away, then what is left of *you?*

The conclusion to the story answers these questions simply: "That is how it is with the man who amasses wealth for himself and remains a pauper in the sight of God" (Luke 12:21).

Why does a man go to business daily? If he goes to get money and nothing else, Jesus would say the trip wasn't worth it. If he goes to get a self, and gets money and a self, that's good. If he gets a self and doesn't get money, that's good too.

The Italian novelist Ignazio Silone, in *Bread and Wine* —a title suggestive of Holy Communion—has a character pointing to Don Simone Scaraffa's villa. "He lived in Brazil for thirty years," said Magascià, "making his fortune out of coffee growing, and came home to enjoy his wealth in peace. So he built that villa. But he went raving mad the first week he lived in it, and had to be taken to the lunatic asylum at Aquila . . . and he's there still. He really might have saved himself the trouble of making his fortune."

When Jesus said you can't serve God and money, he was saying choose your boss—then you will have determined your scale of values, you'll be able to judge what is worth your time and what isn't, you'll know who to take orders from, and how to determine your worth.

Out of this kind of management set-up in our lives we can face our daily decisions. Let me be specific. I received a letter from a faithful and dedicated member of this

congregation who, like so many of us, has made his
ultimate commitment and makes it the pattern for his
business life. I will quote from the letter:

I am a sales engineer, meaning that I have an engineering
background and am engaged in sales work of technical
products. . . . The type of product I sell will fit some machinery and work poorly in other machinery. The real es-
sence of my work is the engineering judgment to distinguish
between them and tell the prospective customer the truth. If
the truth has some qualifications, they must be told also. The
result is that there are many times when I have said that the
product I sell will not be suitable in the proposed machine.
Sometimes I have driven fifty miles to make a special call,
and then found myself telling the man I had nothing to sell
him.

There are two reasons for being frank. First, poor application would only cause later trouble, and cannot be hidden.
My reputation would diminish and I could not make another
sale to that customer. This follows the doctrine "honesty is the
best policy," but this is amoral. Anyway, sometimes it isn't
the best. Second, my engineering and moral judgment would
not permit equivocation. Obviously, the two points reinforce
each other.

On the other hand, there have been occasions when an
unthinking sales manager for whom I worked demanded that
I tell a customer something that I did not think was wholly
true or in the best interests of the customer. I dissembled. I
told the customer exactly what I was instructed to tell,
ascribed it to the sales manager, and then proceeded to
modify the statement with my own views. Sometimes this

type of situation has arisen because the sales manager did not know enough about his own product or the application of it, not because he purposely would mislead. But I have also had sales managers say, "Well, you can lie a little, can't you?" I have taken the view that I can't reform sales managers and have proceeded with customers by my own standards.

An outside salesman, making personal calls on homes or factories, is not subject to close supervision. He can loaf for many hours and pad his expense account wantonly without being discovered. Therefore, a most important quality to seek in hiring such a salesman is integrity.

When my sales contract was broken, I was asked to return all my sales materials to the office. Our written contract was specific about this. It said that sales books and price sheets were to be returned without being copied. I knew that the price information would be valuable to me in the future. I also was sure from much other evidence that the sales manager had not read the contract closely enough to see that clause. So I could have easily gotten away with valuable information. In fact, the sales manager, if he thought about it at all, would have expected me to keep the information because that is what he would have done. I did not. But he wouldn't believe me if I told him that I did not.

Now I have a great deal of sales information on customers and applications that would be valuable to a competitor. I felt I was abused and mistreated by my company, and there was a passing thought that I would give, not sell, the information to a competitior. The thought is gone now. I think that passing along of such trade secrets is a rather common occurrence.

What I got when I read that was the clear picture of a Christian man who is making his daily decisions by an ultimate authority which he has come to hear and understand because of his commitment to Christ. You know as well as I do that a man with no faith at all could, and many do, act exactly the same way as this man, and that is just the point.

The Christian ethic resides not in the act, but in the ultimate loyalty which shapes the act. A man of no faith would act this way as an expression of something—I'm not sure what; but when the Christian man acts the same way, it is the expression of an ultimate commitment.

On Mother's Day a mother may get two corsages exactly alike, one sent by her son and one sent because she was selected at random out of the telephone directory by a disc jockey. The corsages are not the same.

Ethical behavior that looks the same is not the same. Every act of every man's life reflects his ultimate loyalty. It is the loyalty that is important, not the act.

III

It will be instructive for us to look once more at the man history has called "the rich fool"—really, a better title would be "the poor fool."

J. B. Phillips paraphrases this translation: "I'll pull down my barns and build bigger ones where I can store all . . . my goods and I can say to my soul, Soul, you have plenty of good things stored up there for years to come.

. . . But God said to him, 'You fool, this very night you will be asked for *your soul!*'" (Luke 12:18-20.)

The point here is the relationship of the goods he had stored up and his soul. Any man's a fool, whether he has small barns or big barns, or no barns, if he says, "Soul, you have plenty of good things—in the barn or the bank."

It is not that the Christian faith is anti-money. Quite the contrary. There are two famous materialisms in the world; one is the atheistic materialism of Marx, the other is the higher materialism of Jesus Christ.

The whole teaching of the Christian faith gives the material world a real and significant place in the scheme of values. The doctrine of creation declares that the material world was made by God and meant to express glory to his name. The Christian understanding of money and of all forms of wealth is that they are meant to be used as a part of the harmony of life which gives praise to God.

In this sense we are all businessmen. We are of very differing levels of wealth as men count, but we are all generously given the wealth of the creation, of the body, and we all handle some part of God's total resources of energy and brainpower, which produce money to our hands.

Therefore, we are all in danger of the misappropriation of funds—which I take as one of the most serious faults of which a businessman can be guilty. With regard to the creation, the instruments of love, and the power of money, we are trustees for God, not owners. A trust officer in a bank or an investment committee head for a university or a corporation who imagines that the money handled belongs to him is guilty of crime. So are we when we so regard anything God has given us.

To remind us of this regularly, we do a very strange thing in church—in the midst of what some call "spiritual worship," that is to say, music, scripture, prayers, and all the things that make one "feel good." We insinuate the offering. Some of us sit through it as if it had nothing to do with worship. Here is the materialism of the world getting in the way of worship because, we may think, it is a necessary evil. But the offering isn't taken to pay the bills. It is taken because every service of worship is a time when the boss asks his staff how we've done this week with the responsibilities and the assets we've handled for him. And we tell him by the manner in which we participate in this act of worship.

Atheistic materialism says there is no connection between things and God. Christian materialism says there is. We indicate which is our way of life and what is our ultimate commitment by what we do during the offertory.

MINISTRY

MINISTRY: AN EXPLANATION

There is no Conversation Guide for this chapter as for all others. There was considerable conversation, however, around the question of the appropriateness of a chapter on the ministry in a series on lay vocations. This chapter appears here for several reasons.

(1) It is a vocation for laymen. That is to say, all recruits for the ministry come from the laity. If the young read this, they must consider the challenge of the ordained ministry along with all other vocational possibilities. If parents read this, they may be prompted to help their young include the ministry in their vocational considerations.

(2) The great tensions evident in the church at present stem largely from the difference in the way laymen understand the ministry and the way ministers understand the ministry. If laymen who read this book will take a few moments to enter inside one man's understanding of his ministry, it may help them understand their own ministers better. Such understanding would be good for the church.

(3) The new theology is helping us see that the

secular-sacred distinctions are not valid. It is hoped that the presence of this chapter at this place will strengthen the sense of the ministry to which all Christians are called, whether ordained or not.

(4) The insistence that this chapter appear in a volume on lay vocations is, however, very personal. I can't believe anyone enjoys his vocation as I enjoy mine in the ministry of the local church at this particular moment. I wanted to witness to that joy. So here it is.

STATEMENT OF THE ISSUES
by CHARLES M. ("SANDY") HUSS, JR.

At a workcamp in Lapwai, Idaho, I came to know that the phrase "Jesus Christ is Lord and Savior" is not just a pious public truth, but a personal thing to be believed and lived. As I look back upon myself during that experience, I can see a mixed-up kid going to the altar of an Indian gospel camp meeting out of 40 percent emotion and 40 percent guilt reaction. But the other 20 percent was God. Even if I went to the altar for 80 percent the wrong reason, God accepted my action and somehow knew that was what he would have to expect when dealing with me.

Two weeks later I was in Evanston and somehow found my way into Ron Lee's office. Ron was the former minister to youth here at First Methodist Church.

Ron and I talked for hours about the Christian faith, the church, and myself as a person. This was the beginning of my relationship with this church and my call to the ministry. That call didn't come suddenly, but ultimately there did come a point when I could no longer imagine myself doing anything else but being in God's service.

It seems that everyone Ron introduced me to in the church has had some part in the shaping of my life. When I needed a job to stay in high school, Mrs. Olson needed a helper in the kitchen. When my college plans got bogged down, I was fortunate enough to win the Methodist Youth Fellowship scholarship.

There always seemed to be an external confirmation of what I felt inside of me. When I realized that God had a Word for this age, a Word that needed proclaiming, there was always an opportunity—a conference, a meeting, a preaching mission, a rally—always an opportunity to make a personal witness to that Word.

That is what the call to the ministry is—a huge feeling inside of you that the most exciting thing you know is welling up within you, and you must tell the good news to all whom you meet, regardless of the consequences, that your life won't be complete until you have proclaimed this Word. And then you find that it will take your whole life to proclaim it. You find you have the courage to bear, like Stephen, the stones upon your body because your love for God and for his children is greater than any other love you have—greater even than your love for your own earthly body.

The call to the ministry not only gives you the courage of the moment, but also a greater realization of how sadly we have failed God. I am embarking upon years of training and study and preparation, so that I might become ever more sensitive to God's love for the world and man's need for God.

And so I go forth from this church bearing the word of hope and love that I came to know here.

SERMON: ABSURDLY WE DO . . .
Colossians 1:23-29

This is my way of helping to complete, in my poor human flesh, the full tale of Christ's afflictions.—Colossians 1:24

I

Sometimes on a day something jumps up out of the dull routine and grabs hold of the fibers of your mind and won't let go.

Sometimes it happens as you read a book or see a movie, and that's the way it happened to me many weeks ago. The movie was *Becket*. Thomas Becket had been made Archbishop of Canterbury by his boyhood friend King Henry II. This was done almost as a joke, certainly as a political maneuver not taken seriously by either man. But the meaning of this ministry bore in on Becket shaping him into a new man—as it does for most of us. Because Becket takes his new ministry seriously, the friends become enemies. In their last confrontation before the king's men kill the archbishop on the altar of the cathedral, the tension grows intense in their conversation.

And then it happened; a word from Becket flung itself out and stuck: "We must only do—absurdly—what we have been given to do—right to the end."

Absurdly we do—what we are given of God to do.

"Absurdly. That word," said the king, "isn't like you."

"Perhaps. I am no longer like myself," replies Becket.

"I felt for the first time that I was being entrusted with something, that's all—there in that empty cathedral, somewhere in France, that day when you ordered me to take up this burden. I was a man without honor. And suddenly I found it—one I never imagined would ever become mine—the honor of God."

The honor of God—entrusted to me—that is the absurdity which any man who truly understands his ministry feels.

It's what Paul meant when he wrote, "This priceless treasure we hold . . . in a common earthenware jar—to show that the splendid power of it belongs to God and not to us" (II Cor. 4:7 Phillips). What he means is that we are the earthenware jar! "We are imposters who speak the truth," he says in another place (II Cor. 6:8).

II

The absurdity is that the message must go through us!

God, I guess, has his own good reasons for doing it this way.

In choosing a method for communicating the truth about himself, God chose to do it through a person—the person of Christ. Ever since, this has continued as his method—to communicate the truth about himself through human personality. If I had been God, I would have been afraid of it. I would have wanted a more foolproof method than that. But for his own reasons this is the way he decided to do it.

I was seated around a table with a group of theologians. It was hard, sometimes impossible, for me to keep up with their conversation. One man kept talking about the "ambivalence of history." I stopped him and asked him to tell me what he meant by that phrase. He's a man who is always difficult for anybody to understand. This time he was simple enough, and the image has stayed with me. The ambivalence of history is that the absolute truth about God must be transmitted in human life and history, and whenever it is, it is distorted to some extent. It's like, he said, putting a stick half down into water; the part you see through the water seems to be wobbly, twisted, and disjointed from the part that is above the water, clear and straight, but though it is distorted, you know it is the same stick.

That is the ambivalence of history—that is the absurdity of preaching. The absurdity is that if you love me, something of the truth of God comes to you through me. But I am not lovable, so how can you be expected to love me? Or if I seek to become attractive in myself so that you do find me lovable, you, then, love me and not the truth of God.

Are we beginning all over again to produce our credentials? Do we, like some people, need letters of introduction to you, or from you? . . . No, you are all the letter we need. . . . It is plain that you are a letter that has come from Christ, given to us to deliver.

It is in full reliance upon God, through Christ, that we make such claims. There is no question of our being qualified in ourselves: we cannot claim anything as our own. Such qualification as we have comes from God. (II Cor. 3:1-6)

Absurdly we do what God has called us to do—to be window glass full of wobbly, distorting flaws through which the light nonetheless enters.

Part of the absurdity is that, as Paul says, here in Colossians, what is for the whole creation under heaven must narrow down to one man. "This is the gospel which has been proclaimed in the whole creation under heaven; and I, Paul, have become its minister." That which is universal must siphon through the narrow defile of a single person. This must result in the one through whom it passes becoming himself a universal person.

Following the Selma marches David Lawrence commented editorially on the role of the clergy.

Most laymen have always elevated the pastorate to a position of eminence unparalleled by any other profession. . . .

But when a clergyman takes part in a debate on a public question, those who disagree with him feel that he has become a protagonist and that he is himself a participant in controversy. Can members of a congregation feel as friendly or as receptive to a pastor's guidance after they have heard him express views contrary to their own conscientious beliefs?

If the sermons were confined solely to spiritual matters, the layman would accept the interpretation given him as an expression of conscience. . . .

Many clergymen seem to have lost the halo of God's light and to have been plunged into the darkness of life itself. What a tragic loss to the community in which this happens! [1]

Where does Mr. Lawrence think God is all this time? "Lost the halo of God's light . . . plunged into the darkness of life itself." What can he possibly think the Bethlehem manger means but just that! *God himself has plunged into the darkness of life.* And we are to join him. He, thank God for this, is a protagonist, protagonist for man against all evil.

There is considerable talk everywhere these days about

[1] "Is the Clergyman Changing His Role?" (copyrighted editorial), *U. S. News and World Report* (April 19, 1965), p. 116.

94

a split between clergy and laity. A certain amount of this is to be expected. No human being can have passing through his life day after day the larger dimensions of this universal gospel and remain forever shriveled up.

I never feel so authentic as a human being and as a minister as I do when I am standing at the focus of the universality of the gospel—in a church council which represents the unity and oneness of Christ's church, in the work of missions, in the affirmation of Christian brotherhood destroying all barriers of race and color. Anytime any one of us can by his own life witness to the universal elements, he is nearer the truth.

Many politicians have illustrated this difference. A man can be governor or some other state official and be a narrow, sometimes bigoted man, but if he goes to Congress, he usually becomes a changed man. What sounded good on the smaller, hometown stage sounds very different on the world stage.

Another element of absurdity in this ministry is, as Paul says, "It is now my happiness to suffer for you" (Col. 1:24).

There are two kinds of people who get pleasure out of suffering: perverts and Christians. There have been some attempts to psychoanalyze the early Christians and explain them as a group who got a fantastic sexual pleasure out of being persecuted. It is to be admitted that at times the thrill of martyrdom had to be countered by the more stable persons in the Christian church. But not all people who say "it is now my happiness to suffer for you" are abnormal. This is the true mood of a lover or a parent— or a Christian.

Paul—and all ministers—delight to affirm that it is our happiness to suffer for you because "this is my way of helping to complete, in my poor human flesh, the full tale of Christ's afflictions still to be endured, for the sake of his body which is the church" (Col. 1:24).

The suffering to which we are called is not some kind of imagined deprivation of the luxuries of life, nor even the normal wear and tear that goes with any profession which deals with large numbers of people with all human foibles therewith appertaining. Not that. The suffering is of the pattern of the cross: identification with every man until his agony and guilt are real in us and in us meet love and the possibility of redemption.

III

"In baptism . . . you were raised to life with him." (Col. 2:12.)

The ordained ministers who talked with me wanted me to tell you that there is nothing like it. This is the happiest of all vocations.

But the vocation is one to which we are all called. Therefore, the happiness is available to all.

Baptism and confirmation, not ordination, make us all the people of God through whom this whole gospel is delivered in the world to the world. Ordination is what the whole people of God do to set apart a few of us for the purpose of seeing that all the people of God fulfill the ministry given to us all.

Absurdly we do what we are called of God to do.

One of the finest expressions of this absurdity and its accompanying glory is in a poem left by an older preacher:

> I who have given to Thee my best
> Rejoice Thy word is unexpressed.
> And inexpressible must be
> On this side of eternity;
> And I with all my travail vast
> Am glad that I must fail at last.
> If I had found the Word complete
> No glory could I march to meet. . . .
> But now my powers I still must spend
> And go on failing to the end,
> But failing I shall leave behind
> Some hints of the Eternal mind,
> And hungry pilgrims where I went
> May find a broken sacrament." [2]

[2] Edward Shillito, "A Preacher's Thanksgiving."

SCIENCE

CONVERSATION GUIDE

I. The Issues
  A. Define Scientists.
    1. An attitude toward life.
    2. An acceptable vocabulary—not frightened by others.
  B. Training—privilege—responsibilities.
    1. To put special knowledge to use.
    2. To help make the world a better place in which to live. What about the "pure" scientist?
    3. Should scientists suppress new discoveries if they have evil potential? ("As an individual I have every responsibility any community person has, but not special obligations because of science.")
      a. The scientific role of finding it is one thing, but the responsibility for its use is shared by the community.
      b. Scientific discovery is universal and can't be suppressed.
  C. How to spend research funds.

D. Personal issue: Are my beliefs in accord with the church's teachings or am I in danger of being a hypocrite?

E. The church: Are there issues that may be reinterpreted upon which the church takes stands and thereby risks future conflicts, as in the past, when the church opposed the truth?

F. Biologists' work with living organisms.
   1. Animals must be put to death.
   2. There is the possibility of manipulating the nervous system.
   3. To how much manipulation is the scientist entitled?

G. Are matter and spirit the same?
   1. Matter and energy?
   2. The radical difference between the living and the dead.

H. Scientific instruments—designed to sell, known to have certain characteristics and not to have others. This is the problem (as identified the first week by the communications speaker) of "the structured truth."

I. Universities and the problem of "publish or perish" for the sake of continuing research grants.

STATEMENT OF THE ISSUES
by CHARLES A. BERRY

Several weeks ago six of us gathered with Dr. Kirk-patrick to examine and define the moral issues operant in our lives. We were there as representatives of some of the varied specialties encompassed by the broad area of science. We discovered that many of our problems were common to most of the professions and have been discussed previously, but that there were also other issues more peculiar to science itself.

For the most part these may be characterized as moral responsibilities. A basic responsibility is to ourselves. The university academy spends between $15,000 and $150,000 (plus overhead expenses) in training one of us to receive the Ph.D. degree. Is fair value received? Commensurate with the privilege of the granted degree lies the responsibility of putting the special knowledge acquired to the best possible use.

Closely related is the responsibility we bear to our peers and our careers. Those of us within the academic community are employed as teachers as well as researchers. The motto of many universities is short and concise—"Teaching, Research, Service"—inferring that teaching should enjoy top priority since it receives top billing. But many of our associates tell us we must publish or perish, that our hopes for salary advancement and promotion depend primarily upon the quantity of research publications we turn out, less upon the quality of

100

these research efforts, and perhaps not at all upon our functional capacities as teachers. Is it any wonder then that students should complain of being given short shift in the lecture hall and laboratory by faculty people too engrossed in their own experiments to care?

Another of our moral responsibilities should concern each of you—namely, how wisely do we spend your money? Very little research is self-supporting. Most of us rely extensively upon gifts or local and federal grants to support our efforts and to buy our equipment. Sometimes these also pay our salaries. It then becomes our responsibility to spend this money as carefully as if it were our own. But many research projects appear absurd when considered out of context and without adequate background information. Who is to judge whether the expenses of a given research program are merited? Since much research is conducted without the thought of immediate commercial application, we are often placed in the position of seeming to spend your tax dollars simply to satisfy our curiosities.

Another responsibility is that which we bear toward the community. Many of us feel that outside our own specialties our opinion is worth no more than that of any other man on the street. However, the public often acts as if the man bearing the label of scientist has a clearer insight and a more perceptive approach to the problems of the community and the nation. This is not necessarily so, but some of us occasionally forget to doff our expert's mask when we step outside our laboratories.

The contributions of science to our country's technological advancement have been important as well as alarming. The most dramatic example centers around the formulation and development of the atomic and hydrogen bombs. These are terrible instruments of destruction, but they also possess the potential for fruitful and peaceful application. Having been instrumental in the creation of these forces, the scientist must now ask himself what role he should play in their application. Here the guidelines are obscured and the responsibilities undefined.

Those of us who are biologists have still other problems, dealing as we do with living animals. In our research we probe into the nature of life itself, into the living processes. We deal with death and the alterations that occur in matter when the spark of life is gone. Certainly there are moral questions here regarding the sanctity of life.

Finally, the scientist must define his moral position with the church. Much of what the scientist accepts as truth has been contrary to the teachings of the early church. Failure to reconcile the various interpretations of the Word of God with the evidence of the laboratory has led many of our profession to give only hypocritical lip service to religion. Still, who can observe the organization of the universe or the functioning of the body and deny the existence of a supreme architect? Recognition that the work we do in our laboratories contributes to our understanding of the ultimate truth of God is perhaps our greatest moral responsibility.

SERMON: "AS IF . . . GOD'S SPIES"
John 8:31-36

All who are not deaf to truth listen to my voice.—John 18:37

I

Suppose you are a scientist—the kind that works with carbon 14. This skill enables you to test the age of an object. A priest comes to you with a venerated relic—let us say a handkerchief which is reputed to have been used by the disciples to perform miraculous healing. Such accounts are found in Acts. His congregation treasures this relic. It has been the instrument of faith which has exalted many believers. The young priest asks you to put the holy relic to the test of carbon 14.

Would you do it? If your scientific test shows the relic to be only two hundred years old, the faith of many will be affected. A powerful faith force will have gone out of the priest's congregation. Would you do it?

One of our number faced such a request and refused to do it. Within our group we disagreed. Some thought he was right in his sensitivity not to destroy the faith of others by the use of scientific instruments. Others, including the preacher, felt strongly that faith which is based on falsehood is better off upset in the hope that it can be shifted to a base of truth—though one assumes the responsibility for real risk in thus disturbing the faith of another.

Though in our time there is an unmistakable aura of veneration around science, there is, nonetheless, a suspicion of snoopiness. The nonscientific public sometimes feels that the laboratory is prying where man should not look. The scientist occasionally expresses a discomfort with himself for analyzing mysteries—sometimes mysteries which have been central to the sustaining faith of others.

Arthur Compton in the prologue to his book about the discovery at the University of Chicago of the chain reaction which made possible the atomic bomb refers to some ancient legends in this connection.

We all remember Pandora, whose most charming quality was curiosity. Mercury brought her a golden casket which was not to be opened, but, of course, she opened it, releasing a swarm of insects—suspicion, hatred, fear, and malice. She quickly closed the top back. Then she began to hear a voice from inside demanding that she open it a second time. She did and then came a lovely butterfly—hope. There is also the story of Prometheus, who stole fire from the gods to give it to men. As punishment for his audacity he was chained to a mountain. A vulture constantly tore at his ever renewing liver.

But it is to King Lear that I would have us turn. Lear, who with his daughter Cordelia faces the unpromising end of their tragedy, lifts a noble attitude toward life as they are taken off to prison:

So we'll live,
And pray, and sing, and tell old tales, and laugh . . .
And take upon 's the mystery of things,
As if we were God's spies.

II

We are all meant to be spies—searching in the mystery of things for God's truth.

Science is a branch of that search. There are men of science who come to church regularly but confess that they are uncomfortable for fear they are guilty of hypocrisy. Such a man knows himself to possess an inquiring mind. He has been trained to ask questions, to accept nothing on faith. It is reported that Einstein was asked how he came to uncover the theory of relativity. He replied, "I challenged an axiom."

If a man whose daily business it is to be skeptical, to ask always for experimentation and proof, comes to church, is he out of character? If the church stands for dogmatism, yes. If attendance at church means acceptance of the crimes against truth which the church has in its history committed, yes.

But is faith opposed to search? Or is it too a search for truth? Emily Dickinson wrote:

> Faith is a fine invention
> For gentlemen who see;
> But microscopes are prudent
> In an emergency.

Surely this is not as difficult as we always make it. The so-called conflict between science and religion is continuously in our conversations and is clearly thought of as a major problem for modern man. It seems clear to me that there is no such problem. I think we are not guilty of oversimplification if we accept the following propositions:

1. The church over and over again has been unfaithful to the truth as indeed science in its practice has just as often been guilty of being unfaithful to the truth. The histories of the church and of science are both full of quackery.

2. Truth is a unity. The one truth is the object of the search of man, scientific and religious.

3. All truth cannot be discovered by any one faculty in man's possession. This is the point at which a conflict between science and religion may develop if a person thinks that all truth can be discovered by one faculty alone. That is, if you believe that man's reason is capable eventually of uncovering all truth, then you'll come into conflict with the claims of religious faith. This kind of thinking sees all discoveries of man's mind as territory which has been discovered by explorers. All around the edges of the truth is the unknown—and that is the area of religious faith and superstition. But it too, one day, will be explored until finally there is no need for any truth to remain uncovered by reason.

I say if you believe that, then there is no hope of avoiding a conflict with religious faith. The reverse position is held by some—that faith is the one and only method of arriving at truth, and reason is not at all dependable. This is as hopeless as the former attitude.

4. Rather, it seems to me, the Christian viewpoint is that all truth is a unity. That some parts of it can be uncovered by reason, and some must be arrived at through faith. That this will always be the case. That faith is not incompleted reason, but that the nature of the ultimate truth is such that it is unknowable by the reason and must be known by faith.

5. Thus science and the church are equally under the judgment of the ultimate truth. Neither must go against the ultimate truth.

6. The scientist as scientist can't know this. As scientist he must only credit the truth which is provided by reason, but the scientist as scientist is only part of a man. The scientist as man can know and accept the larger principles of truth without being unfaithful to the narrow principles of his discipline.

The scientist is engaged in the awesome task of describing the universe. As he enlarges the picture, man is called on to adjust his living patterns to take into account the new facts.

Life is different for us because we know how far it is to the moon, the sun, and the stars. Because we can telephone instead of having to go in person to talk. Because we can fly to New York from Chicago in an hour and a half. Because satellites throw television pictures from one continent to another. Because the power of the atom has been released. Because the inner workings of the body are becoming more and more known.

The spirit of the man who must change the mode of his life because of the new dimensions of the world he lives in is deeply affected by the new knowledge. This is the point where many of the difficult questions which face the practicing scientist focus.

Does he bear guilt for uncovering new truth which results in widespread evil? The problem is that Dr. Jekyll and Mr. Hyde have become Dr. Jekyll and Dr. Hyde. Aldous Huxley in *The Genius and the Goddess* has the young scientist John Rivers says, "Those were the days, remember, when you could be a physicist without feeling guilty; the days when it was still possible to believe that you were working for the greater glory of God. Now they won't even allow you the comfort of self-deception. You're paid by the Navy and trailed by the F.B.I. Not for one moment do they permit you to forget what you're up to. *Ad majorem Dei gloriam?* Don't be an idiot! *Ad majorem hominis degradationem*—that's the thing you're working for."

Or if this is not the point for guilt, it becomes the point for pride. Having discovered some of God's new truth, the discoverer easily mistakes himself for God. It is not easy for any of us to come to know something new without falling into pride.

The story of God's casting the first man out of Eden illuminates this fall. There is something about being a man which is different from being a god. There were

108

two trees in the garden—the tree of life and the tree of the knowledge of good and evil. Man can only eat of one; only God eats of both.

What, then, is the answer for the man who engages in the awesome task of describing the universe? How does he avoid guilt and pride? The Christian faith declares that there is an additional set of facts. They are faith facts. When they are combined with reason facts, only then is a human being complete.

It is an insight which cannot be ignored that facts are not the truth. Any set of facts must be interpreted. The interpretation makes the difference between truth and falsity.

Faith is an interpretation of the facts, an interpretation which some men believe produces the truth. That is to say that the universe which the scientist describes is looked at by the man of faith, and he produces a Christian world view: a view that connects the Maker of the universe with the Judge of the universe with the Lover of the universe. No scientist describes the universe that way, but some men of faith looking at the scientist's description see it that way. Are they right or wrong? No one knows. No one can prove them right. No one can prove them wrong. They are men who have chosen to live on the basis of that interpretation of the facts.

Every man chooses his interpretation of the facts and lives by it. Every man does that. The question is: Which faith will you use as your faith interpretation of the facts?

III

Jesus talked about the truth in several places. He said, "If you dwell within the revelation I have brought, you are indeed my disciples; you shall know the truth, and the truth will set you free" (John 8:31-32). That is, Jesus Christ represents a point of view toward this whole universe and life in it. If a man takes that viewpoint and lives by it, he can live a released life in this universe—he can be free.

When his life was at stake Jesus said to Pilate, the judge: "My business in this world is to stand for the truth. For this was I born; for this I came into the world, and *all who are not deaf to truth listen to my voice.*"

That is to say, if a scientist or a student or any man is dedicated to finding the truth—the whole truth—he will want to listen to and to experiment with the viewpoint Jesus brought with regard to living in this universe, this universe which man's reason is increasingly uncovering.

Listen again to Arthur Compton: "Christianity has the key to survival and the good life in the modern world. Others also have found this key. From whatever source the affirmation of man's inborn worth may come, those for whom this is a basic principle of action are welcome partners in the great cause of freedom. But my own acceptance of this view of man stems directly from Jesus' teaching." [1]

[1] *Atomic Quest* (New York: Oxford Univ. Press, 1956), p. 344.

110

To accept Jesus' viewpoint as our faith interpretation of the world is to accept certain commitments for our lives—moral commitments. This is one reason why many of us would like to live in the world of reason alone. We think we can do so and meet the demands of reason. But to accept Christ is to be confronted with larger demands we are slow to accept.

To quote Arthur Compton once more:

This recognition of a kind of kinship with the Creator-God is for me a matter of vital importance. The opportunity to share with God the shaping of the conditions of life is a tremendous challenge and the great responsibility that comes with freedom. To be able to say, "My Father is working toward this goal, and I am sharing in His task," is the highest level of activity to which I as a Christian can aspire. This realization of responsible partnership with God gives me inspiration and courage to undertake great tasks. And the greatest of these tasks, as I see it, is to make it possible also for others who are equally God's children to do their responsible share.[2]

This is the place of the choice of ultimate meaning. There are those of us who believe that the happiest, most meaningful way to live in the new world—or any other yet to be uncovered—is the way of living which emerges from understanding life and the universe the way Jesus explained it by his own life on this planet.

[2] *Ibid.*, p. 345.

111

There is, I am happy to discover, a hymn appropriate to the Space Age.

> And have the bright immensities
>   Received our risen Lord,
> Where light-years frame the Pleiades
>   And point Orion's sword?
> Do flaming suns his footsteps trace
>   Through corridors sublime,
> The Lord of interstellar space
>   And conqueror of time? [3]

It is up to us to see that the church in our time is never guilty of the crimes of the past, of being arrayed with falsehood against truth. Nor will we allow the naïve to surrender the reality of faith to the supremacy of reason. Rather, we will bring both the church and the laboratory under the judgment of truth, and into the fullest contribution to meaning each can make.

> The heaven that hides him from our sight
>   Knows neither near nor far:
> An altar candle sheds its light
>   As surely as a star;
> And where his loving people meet
>   To share the gift divine,
> There stands he with unhurrying feet;
>   There heavenly splendors shine. [4]

[3] Howard Chandler Robbins, "And Have the Bright Immensities," *Way of Light* (New York: Morehouse Publishing Co., 1933).
[4] *Ibid.*

PUBLIC SERVICE

CONVERSATION GUIDE

I. The Issues

  A. We must recognize the difference in the purpose of a public organization which exists for service and the purpose of business organizations which exist for profit (or for themselves).

  B. The question of accountability to the public with the difficulty of determining the mind of the public.

    1. What to do when one's own personal beliefs differ from the public consensus which one represents.

    2. Government policies affect people's individual lives.

      a. The employee bears the brunt of reactions and criticisms of the policy.

      b. The employee may also object to the growing power of government, but at the same time be a part of it.

      c. The public benefit is difficult to determine (such as in the case of cutting down beautiful trees to build an expressway).

   C. What is "able" administration in relation to the public?

      1. Responsibility for information being disseminated. How does this differ from an indefensible kind of public relations stance?

      2. Should the employee or appointee attempt to influence the policy-making board?

      3. What to do in case of conflicts. How to determine where a man's survival line is.

   D. What does the Christian conscience say about dealing with people en masse rather than as individuals? Is the church interested only in individuals or also in the results of individuals in social situations?

   E. What does the individual Christian do when he finds himself at variance with pronouncements of his church in the field of his operation? On matters of theology?

      1. Soldier in Vietnam.

      2. Police action in racial disturbances.

      3. City official issuing liquor licenses.

II. Scripture to look at for direction

    Deuteronomy 1:9-18

    Righteousness the foundation of the city; judgment on the city for unrighteousness: Proverbs 14:34; Isaiah 32:1-8, 17-20; Amos 5

    Subject to higher powers; honor of rulers: Romans 13:1-6; Titus 3:1; I Peter 2:13-14

    Story of Joseph: Genesis 41–50

Jesus paying taxes: Matthew 17:24-27
Render to Caesar: Matthew 22:15-22

STATEMENT OF THE ISSUES
by ARMON LUND

If man is to find what many consider the good life—
some say he already has—apparently he will have to find
it in the city. There is no escape. With more than 70
percent of the people in America residing in cities, and
more coming, the public administrator must call on all the
resources of technology and the social sciences to create
an urban climate helpful to man in his search for the
millennium.

Eighteenth-century American political leaders took
their conception of man from the central religious tradi-
tions of western civilization. They insisted that the individual man belonged to his creator, and since his was
an immortal soul, he was entitled to certain inalienable
rights which no government, here or elsewhere, had the
right to deny him.

This is what has been called the "forgotten foundation
of democracy." But although it may have been forgotten,
it is not lost.

Today's public administrator feels that he has an un-
equaled opportunity to contribute to the welfare of
society in a broad and difficult field, and to turn ideals
into realities. Possibly his greatest contribution is toward

the preservation of the ideals upon which our government is based: equal treatment under the law and equal opportunity for all men.

One of the most important tasks in America today is that of improving public service, especially in the field of local government.

In America's surging growth of urbanism both abundance and blight have sprawled across the land. In wake of that surge are cluttered landscapes; polluted air and water; congested transportation; inadequate schools, housing, and recreational facilities; and conflicting, overlapping jurisdictions in governmental patterns. We are beset with a rapidly expanding population whose anxieties, often paradoxical and overwhelming, frequently find expression in the behavior of youth and adults, eroding and destroying human values and physical resources and curtailing human development and fulfillment.

But cities and urban areas are also where man desires to live and where with accelerating pace he is congregating. It is in urban areas that most of our universities, research centers, museums, and libraries are located; where literacy is high; where man finds maximum opportunities for intellectual growth.

It is in urban areas where industrial and commercial enterprise are located and where through creative technology gainful employment is available.

It is in urban areas where virtually all the nation's music centers, art galleries, and creative workshops thrive and afford opportunity for cultural development.

116

It is in urban areas where men of all ethnic and cultural origins congregate and where man discovers his finest opportunity to learn of the richness, diversity, and individuality of his fellowman and of his responsibility as a citizen.

It is in the urban areas, these man-built centers, that man feels closest to his governmental officials and that government services are most immediate and direct.

In these urban areas man's communication with public administrators is most diverse and most frequent. Here man fulfills most of his governmental needs in a relationship which can be intimate, friendly, and personal.

In such an environment, geared to a fast-changing, expanding, and complex society, an environment where man is confronted daily with new problems and with many old ones still unsolved, the ethical and moral standards which the administrator sets for himself must fulfill his social responsibility as a trusted public servant.

SERMON: AT YOUR SERVICE
Genesis 41:25, 29-44

Can we find such a man as this, in whom is the Spirit of God?
—Genesis 41:38

I

"Bureaucrats" . . . "selfish politicians" . . . "clock watchers" . . . "red tape." . . . "Why don't we have better people in government?" "Why don't we clean up politics?" This is the rather sharp way the Ford Foundation begins its report on its work in the field of public service. Then it answers with a more rational comment:

At times in the nation's history the epithets and questions flung by Americans at their government have ranged from close approximations to gross exaggerations of the facts. But today thoughtful students of public affairs are convinced that the nation can ill afford the luxury of the stereotypes, the disdain and indifference toward public service that they imply, and whatever reality they may reflect. . . .

While much can be said and has been done within government to improve its effectiveness and attractiveness, a key responsibility rests with the citizen, who sanctions government, and for whom is government's reason for being in a free society.[1]

The tone and direction of the entire report is set by a quotation from Elihu Root on the cover: "Politics is the practical exercise of the art of self-government and somebody must attend to it if we are to have self-government."

Once again I have benefited from the willingness of a group of laymen in this church who took time for two sessions with their preacher. We talked about the things they face in the daily performance of their lives as public servants.

[1] "Skills, Scholarship and the Public Service" (a Ford Foundation Report, April, 1966), p. 3.

It doesn't appear to me that we have as many persons engaged in public service vocations as in some others. We do have city employees, aldermen, teachers and administrators in the school system, police, and persons on staffs of agencies responsible to some branch of government. Among these persons are those who are elected by the public and those appointed by the persons elected.

Whether the number of persons engaged in such vocations is very large or not, the issues and problems connected with this area of human endeavor are important to us all. As citizens we are all affected by, and we in turn affect, the conduct of persons whose vocational lives are spent in public service. "A key responsibility rests with the citizen, who sanctions government, and for whom government exists," says the Ford Foundation report.

One of the first things we must recognize ought to be obvious, but it isn't. That is that the differing structures of human organization have different purposes. Business exists for profit; government and many other organizations do not. It makes a difference in the conduct of a vocation whether one's organization exists for itself or for service to others.

The fact that constituents don't always understand this makes many difficulties for the public servant, and opens up one of his major areas of vocational frustration.

That is the question of accountability. It seemed to me as I listened to these persons talk that almost all questions come back to this basic one: To whom am I accountable? To most of us I guess the answer would seem obvious and simple: the public.

But who is the public? And how does one determine the mind of the public? Which segment does one listen to, for on any issue there will be divergent minds in the public. Even if a significant proportion of the public seems to be of one mind, is it necessarily the best for the public in the long run? Does the fact that an administrator may have a broader viewpoint and access to more information force him at times to do for the public what the public doesn't want? For example, should trees be cut down to build roads? Is the public servant accountable only to the public, or is he in some sense responsible for his own integrity? Above all, is a person accountable to God for the conduct of his daily life in public service? If at any one time his obligation to the public, to his own integrity, and to God all add up to the same thing, he is a lucky man and will have a good day that day. But what of the other days?

I won't restate the other issues; that has been well done by Armon Lund. But I will come at them in an effort to find some basic principles of guidance in the whole area of vocational public service and the citizen's attitude toward his government and its employees.

II

You'll find it strange, I'm sure, that I should turn to the book of Genesis for a scriptural base to this sermon.

What can a man be thinking about who will try to deal with modern government by turning to the Old Testament? Simply this: the church is that group of people who believe that in this body of literature there are universal principles which address themselves to man in his essential life. To be a Christian is to be committed to the effort to understand all of life in the light of these universal principles. It is to acknowledge, in fact, that we are judged by them and must answer to them.

In this regard I have been unable to put Joseph out of my mind during the whole process of thinking on these questions. For most of my life his biography has been one of the most fascinating in print. I hope it may become so for you sometime.

Joseph became prime minister in the government of Egypt under one of the pharaohs. This was quite an achievement in view of the fact that he was a foreigner, a Jew (a fact which wasn't any more help then in gaining public office than it is now).

He was in his youth evidently a very overbearing, conceited person. His brothers were so inflamed by this and by their own jealousy that they almost killed him. They decided to sell him into slavery instead. That resulted in his being transported from his own country into Egypt.

He had an amazing amount of natural ability, for more than once when he was on the very bottom he shot quickly to the top. In jail on one occasion his cellmates were two servants from the court. He analyzed their dreams. One servant was beheaded; the other got his job back. The servant who had been restored had promised to return the favor, but promptly forgot about his old friend. (That's enough to prove that this story is as contemporary as modern machine politics.)

The day came when the king had a dream; after everybody else had tried and failed to interpret it, the butler remembered his friend Joseph. So Joseph was brought out of prison. His analysis of the economic projections for the next fourteen years and of the kind of administrator the king needed to be in charge was so brilliant that the pharaoh asked: "Can we find such a man as this?" Then, with no personnel department to make surveys, he did the obvious thing: "Since God has shown you all this, there is none so discreet and wise as you are." He made him second in command: executive vice-pharaoh.

There are two other incidents we should call to mind —one earlier and one later. The earlier one was when the wife of his boss tried to seduce him into an affair with her. He resisted; this angered her, and she framed him. That's why he was in prison in the first place. Then much later, after he had the economy under control so that periods of affluence offset the period of famine, his brothers came to Egypt for help in the time of their famine. They still lived in a land of completely free economy. When they came to him for help, they didn't recognize him, but he recognized them.

You'll have to read the details for yourself. But here is a picture of a man who helps us today at some very fundamental points.

First, in dealing with people under his government he administered policies that were intended to be for the benefit of all. He would not give in under pressure even though giving in would have eased his situation. To give in would have been unfair to the public.

Our friends confess that it wears a person down to be at the center where reactions and criticisms of the government always come. Their telephones ring, and they must take personally the abuse the caller feels toward his government's actions.

Joseph was dealing with people who wanted to say, "It's my farm; it's my sweat; why isn't it my crop?" "Look at the surplus that fellow is piling up. So much they've lost count of how much." "He's probably eating it himself and giving special rations to his cronies." This is the kind of thing he had to put up with during the seven fat years. In the following lean years we can all imagine the pressures and criticisms. He was just lucky telephones hadn't been invented in those days!

Public servants must include in their commitment to service the willingness to bear this kind of burden. No one can redefine the job to avoid it. We who are citizens can support them with our understanding and, most of all, our confidence. I have never had such a response to a sermon as to one I recently preached on "What Happened to Trust?" I have wondered why. Is it because we all are ready to admit that we have been guilty of accusing other people falsely? Or is it because we all feel ourselves victims of this unfairness? I suspect the latter.

So we must recommit ourselves to an understanding of what is called for when we decide to live together. It means we must surrender some of our own personal desires and control to the larger body politic. He who must administer it must accept the responsibility of it. It will wear him down by the end of the day, but he must yet find inner pride and peace in knowing that he has done what he is called to do to make it possible for people to live together.

Second, in dealing with those who had wronged him Joseph gave us the ideal model for all such dealings.

Read the story. It is a tender, moving portrayal. We all know the problem of dealing with hurts that others inflict on us. The natural urge of our lower selves is to retaliate. When a person in this situation is possessed of tremendous power, the temptation is almost beyond resisting. A powerful factor in holding Joseph steady was the fact that he recognized these men as his brothers. Many times we are all thrown into a conflict in which the other person doesn't act like a brother should, doesn't recognize the relationship. Are we, therefore, obligated to perform a one-way brotherhood? The answer is yes, if we want to be true to the Christian way of life and to the God who is the Father of all people.

124

We must remember that there are so many times when the circumstances themselves do not obviously define a relationship of brotherhood. Then it is up to the person who seeks to preserve his own Christian definition of his relationships to act as a true brother whether the other party does or not. Let us acknowledge that whenever we find one in public life with such largeness of spirit as is here manifest, the total citizenry is fortunate.

Third, in dealing with his own integrity Joseph shows us what it is like to be a person who is willing to pay the price to maintain his own true selfhood.

In professions in which the administrator is largely dependent on the persuasion of others, there is always a legitimate place for compromise. In fact, such persons are obligated to a certain amount and type of compromise to move the constituency along. If a public administrator does not have a lot of give and take, he will block the processes which enable people to make up their minds, and sometimes to change them. A changed constituency won't result if the administrator always insists on getting his way about everything. But compromise is a word we use negatively so often that a person who engages in it will always be criticized by someone. And it is well that we criticize compromise, at least that we keep a very watchful eye on it at all times, for there are issues which cannot and must not be compromised.

This means that every public servant must know himself well enough to know where two lines are: (1) The integrity line. Every person must know where the line is beyond which he will not go, but up to which he is flexible for the good of the whole. (2) The survival line. A wise public servant knows instinctively where this line is and that if he crosses it, he's finished. He's a fortunate man if he can keep these two lines close to each other.

Fourth, in all his dealing Joseph saw himself as primarily accountable to God. Such an undergirding for one's vocation is invaluable. Keeping a due sense of humility about it, the Christian must nonetheless have the quiet but strong confidence that the performance of his public service in accordance with the will and purpose of God is after all, and ultimately, in the best interests of the public.

III

Numerous scriptural passages declare that the only solid base of a city or a nation is righteousness—*but what is righteousness?*

Some of the most agonizing decisions result from the fact that persons equally committed to governing a city or a nation on the basis of righteousness may hold diametrically opposed definitions of what is right.

War is wrong. Most everybody would agree to that. A nation ought to be peace-loving. We all agree. The world is better off if we can maintain peace. But was World War I wrong? And World War II? And the Korean War? And the present war in Vietnam? The President insists that the only righteous thing to do is to pursue a policy of war; his critics call for peace as the only righteous policy.

So it is never enough for us to say that the public servant must do what is right. We must find ways to help him define what is right. What are some of the sources of this kind of help?

Information—as much as a person can gather, from as many varying points of view as possible. We live in a world in which this is no problem. We must all support the free flow of information. And the public servant must beware of the temptation to use these free channels to manipulate the information available to the public. We must be committed to the confidence that the people must be allowed to know all the facts.

But something more than information is needed, for facts often exist in abundance on both sides of a question. A person needs moral guidance. Here again we live in a fortunate time. The churches are exceedingly active in seeking to fulfill this role. Denominations and councils of churches bring together large numbers of knowledge-able people, knowledgeable both in the facts of the world and in the theological and ethical principles of the faith. It is a combination we all need to have guiding us with resolutions and pronouncements.

For example, praise has come from top officials at both the national and state level for the social creed of The Methodist Church. President Lyndon Johnson quoted extensively from the creed in his address to the Bicentennial Celebration of Methodism in Baltimore and asserted that "it would be hard to write a more perfect description of the American ideal—or of the American commitment in the 1960's." Governor Breathitt of Kentucky is quoted as having told the Council of Bishops that the creed would be a good guide for the governor of any state to follow on social concerns. "The closing paragraph of the social creed offers to us all a clear mandate to read, study, and then apply in actual living the underlying principles of our Methodist heritage," the governor said. "I tell you, it's a pretty good mandate to follow as a governor of a state."

But what is a good churchman to do and feel if his church takes one stand and he must take the opposite in his practical decisions? For example, the aldermen of Evanston must vote on ordinances designed to correct the present racial discrimination in housing which exists in our town. Perhaps all of them are members of churches which are on record as favoring the kind of action they may vote against.

What are the soldier in Vietnam and his family to think when their church and church leaders protest the action there as unchristian?

It all points each one of us back to the basic fact of life and of the Christian life: There is an ultimate point of aloneness where each one of us is forced by life—there we must choose. We are obligated not to choose as someone else wants us to but to have some clear principles, tried and tested at other times, by which we acknowledge our accountability to God, to the community of believers, to the church, to our own personal integrity, and to the larger community—who may or may not understand, and who may or may not fire us!

WOMEN

CONVERSATION GUIDE

I. The Issues
  A. Family/career choice.
   1. In earlier generations it was thought that a family was the fulfillment of a woman's nature; in our time there is widespread expression of the attitude that a family may hinder fulfillment, which is thought to come from freedom to fulfill a career.
      a. How does a woman choose between family and career?
      b. What are the standards of fulfillment in each?
      c. How can a woman handle disappointment if the one she wants is not offered?
      d. How can she combine them, if necessary? How can she determine that it is necessary?
   2. The problem of wasted womanpower and the either-or proposition that stands between a woman and the acceptance of herself as a person.
   3. What happens to the family in a two-income earner situation? What about the definition of the role of the man in such cases?

130

B. Family situations.
   1. The daily relationship with husband, children, other family members, and friends.
   2. Remaining active and interesting though not working outside the home.
   3. Relations with neighbors and conflicts of moral standards, especially in guiding children in their values.
   4. Seeing children as individuals and not as extensions of oneself, while keeping authority as parent.
C. Career situations.
   1. Difference between women and men in making choices: with women decisions tend to be seen as black and white; men seem to accommodate themselves to choices in the gray area.
   2. School training is oriented toward a job rather than motherhood.
   3. What changes are called forth in a feminine personality by advancement to equality in executive opportunities?
D. Concern about:
   1. Sickness, death, decisions, loneliness, and discouragement. Different for women than for men? Woman's orientation is more physical—concern for the health of the family, proper food, and other physical necessities.
   2. The woman who must live in a nonfamily situation.

      a. Economic pressure to accept an unacceptable marriage.

      b. The need for group life.

   E. The modern use of woman as a commodity.

     1. Sex symbol.

     2. Trying to live up to the TV image while shouldering the mundane tasks of home and family life.

II. Beginning Thoughts

   A. Are any significant differences between men and women theologically based? If so, does this mean that they must be maintained? Are there changes taking place in the nature of women, brought about by the pressures of the times toward equality? Good or bad?

   B. Are there needs for a certain type of religious faith for women, one to meet their own distinctive needs?

   C. Is the acceptance of a distinctive role necessarily a secondary role?

   D. Is there a Christian doctrine of sex?

   E. Should women play a distinctive role in maintaining standards of morality? Can they do so? What are the forces working toward the "new morality"?

   F. Any modern validity in biblical women? Eve, Delilah, Mary, Mary Magdalene, etc.

III. Scripture to look at for direction

   Proverbs 31:10-31

   Ministries listed in scripture as performed by women:

     Hospitality to the prophet: II Kings 4:8-10

     Kindness to the poor: Proverbs 31:20

Contributing to Christ's comfort: Matthew 27:55;
  Mark 14:3-9; Luke 7:37-39
Serving the church: Romans 16:1-2
Co-laborers with Paul: Romans 16:3-4, 6, 12

STATEMENT OF THE ISSUES
by MRS. J. ROBERT GETTEL

When Dr. Kirkpatrick asked me to make this statement, I told him I felt it would probably detract from
and certainly not add to his sermon. However, he wanted
you to have before you the issues which came from our
discussion of some of the times when women most feel
the need of a strong, sustaining faith. Several women of
the church contributed to this discussion. Our questions
arose from the consideration of a woman's vocation, her
calling to and occupation with homemaking or a career
or both.

We started with the premise that in earlier generations
it was thought that a family was the fulfillment of a
woman's nature; in our time there is a widespread attitude that family may hinder fulfillment, which is thought
to come from freedom to fulfill a career. These questions
came to mind:

How does a woman choose between marriage and
family or a career?

What are the standards of fulfillment in each?

133

How can she handle disappointment if the choice she wants is not offered?

How does she combine attention to both family and career, if necessary?

Specific questions of concern to the woman who is a wife and mother were as follows: What bearing does a woman's faith have upon her family relationship with her husband, children, other family members, and friends? Her relations with neighbors and conflicts in moral standards, especially in the guiding of children in their values? Helping her children become individuals and not extensions of herself, while still keeping her authority as a parent? Remaining active and interesting, though not working outside the home, and adjusting to marriage and motherhood when her school training has been oriented toward a job?

In examining some of the rough spots where women pursuing careers may especially need faith, we considered the following:

Since a woman supposedly sees choices in terms of black and white, can she adjust in a man's job world to complex shaded decisions?

How does the single woman fulfill her need for group life?

If a middle-aged woman must live in a nonfamily situation, how does she overcome loneliness which sometimes tends to pressure her into making a bad marriage?

Lastly, these were the issues of concern to all women:

How does the Christian woman feel about the modern use of woman as a commodity?

Does she wish to be a sex symbol?

Does she want to live up to the TV image?

Are women generally more or differently concerned about sickness, death, decisions, loneliness, and discouragement than men?

Does a woman have a special role with regard to religion and the maintenance of standards of morality?

SERMON: THE PROVERBIAL WOMAN
Proverbs 31:10-31

Charm is deceitful, and beauty is vain.—Proverbs 31:30

I

Bishop Warren Candler used to say, "Boys, just because God made Eve out of Adam's rib, don't think women are a side issue!" In a vocational series it should be no surprise to find one sermon devoted to women. For it is quite clear, given as much as a moment's thought, that being a woman raises special vocational and faith questions, as surely as being a scientist or a lawyer does. She is no side issue!

In our group meeting we discovered that, whether it helps or not, the Scriptures give extensive and ample attention to women. To mention a few: Eve, Sarah, Rebekah, Rachel, Miriam, Deborah, Ruth, Hannah, Rahab,

135

Esther, Delilah, Jezebel, Mary Magdalene, Mary the mother of Jesus, Mary the sister of Martha, Dorcas, Lydia, Phoebe, Priscilla.

We turn now to Proverbs. Not to the many verses where young men are warned against wicked women, but to the finest of all statements in "Praise of a Worthy Woman," a poem which has been called the "golden ABC's of the perfect wife." It is called the "golden ABC's" because that is literally what these closing verses of the book of Proverbs are. They are an acrostic—each of these twenty-two verses begins with a letter of the Hebrew alphabet in consecutive order. Thus, the whole alphabet is literally summoned to expound the virtues of a worthy woman.

And that's where our problem with Scripture begins— it's a bit too neat. Is this writer describing a real live human being, or is he playing with a clever scheme on paper? That's our danger too.

No woman here would recognize herself in this description. Not that you have failed to reach the level of perfection here described, but if you had, as specifically outlined, you would not be a worthy modern woman. For the woman described in Proverbs is not the woman any one of you wants to be.

That is true of any proverbial woman anyone could describe. She is not you. When we talk here we must generalize, but no woman is a generalized woman.

I point this out—and have purposely chosen the sermon

title to emphasize it—so that if you know that I know this, you may again be reminded that worship must be dialogue. The preacher can only generalize; every hearer must particularize.

The business of making the Christian faith relevant to the next six days is your task. The points where you begin, it seems to me, are these.

II

"Charm is deceitful and beauty is vain, but a woman who fears the Lord is to be praised."

Now let's not get off on the wrong foot right from the start. Let me make it quite clear, I'm prejudiced in favor of beautiful, charming women as over against any other kind.

When I was a boy and my mother and I talked about girls, she insisted, as does the writer of these proverbs, that the important thing is not good looks, but a good girl. I agreed, but insisted that somewhere there must be a good-looking, good girl.

In regard to the verse from Proverbs, the English reading which comes out "fear of the Lord" is not to be thought of as the cringing terror we so often use the word "fear" to express. More properly it is what we mean by the word "reverence." Some more modern translations make this clear—for example, J. M. P. Smith's "Reverence for the Lord is the beginning of knowledge"

(Prov. 1:7) and "a woman who reveres the Lord—she will be praised" (Prov. 31:30).

Dr. Harris Franklin Rall wrote, "Reverence is the response of the soul in the presence of that which has not only power but worth. It is the soul's attitude toward that God in whom goodness and power are one. It is stirred in man whenever he finds those values which he counts as holy, to whose acknowledged claim all else must yield." [1]

Without that in a woman, any charm she may have is deceitful and any beauty is vain. A woman who reverences or who acknowledges God's claim as that to which all else must yield, who has that at the center and clothes it in charm and beauty, is God's finest creation, equaled by nothing else he has made. Such a woman's children rise up and call her blessed (not till they get through the teens) and her husband also, and he praises her (though she may have trouble getting the words out of him on some days).

> Many women have done excellently,
> but you surpass them all. . . .
> Give her of the fruit of her hands,
> and let her works praise her in the gates.
> (Prov. 31:29, 31)

But how does a woman come to such a central faith? There was a time when we just assumed that faith was

[1] *Christianity* (New York: Charles Scribner's Sons, 1940), p. 11.

an instinct of the female, that it suited her nature to be religious. You couldn't expect it of men—unless they tended to be effeminate—but women had it without any effort.

If that were ever true, surely no one supposes it to be so any more. One of the ladies furnished me with several articles written by women about themselves. One began this way: "To find faith is a frustrating thing in these days geared to pressing a button and getting instant results." [2] And the other began with lines by Saul Bass in a documentary film shown at the New York World's Fair:

> The more we are able to see, the more we look for.
> The more we question, the more there is to question.
> The more we experience, the more we want to experience.
> The more we comtemplate, the greater our need for
> contemplation. [3]

How does she come to faith? How does she become this very worthy person?

When we look again at this proverbial woman, or this woman described in Proverbs, with modern eyes, we will be surprised to discover that she is defined by the things she does. All these verses tell of things she does:

> She seeks wool and flax,
> and works with willing hands. . . .

[2] Frances Routsong, "Faith—the Force of Life," *The PEO Record* (February, 1965), p. 10.
[3] Myrtle R. Doolittle, "No Vision But Faith," *The PEO Record* (March, 1965), p. 12.

> She rises while it is yet night
>> and provides food for her household. . . .
> She puts her hands to the distaff,
>> and her hands hold the spindle. . . .
> She looks well to the ways of her household,
>> and does not eat the bread of idleness.

This doesn't say a thing about her feminine mystique or about becoming a self. It was written in a world that knew nothing about career women and the freedom of self-expression.

The modern woman's world is vastly different; no one would recommend a reversion to this, but look more deeply at what may be eternal (that is to say, contemporary) wisdom here.

The woman is defined *at* the point of what she does and the faithful manner in which she does it, but she is defined *by* the attitude and reason she holds for doing it. Her attitude and reason are shaped by her relationships. She does these things well because she is doing them for her family and others.

The modern woman is busy too—although not at the same kinds of tasks. But she is as busy as this woman of Proverbs. If the modern woman fails to find meaning and purpose for herself in what she does, it may be because she has failed to make the connection between all she is doing and her relationships with others.

It is a basic truth of faith that we only develop a true and meaningful selfhood in our relationships with others.

The family relationship is the one none of us can

avoid. Nobody ever came into life without it in some form. We can renounce it, but we can't avoid coming into life through it. This God has determined in the hope that, having been forced into at least one context of relationships, we may discover the fundamental lesson of life: that all meaning is to be discovered in relationships.

After the first family is forced on us, we are then free to choose whether there will be a second family. I could not avoid being a son, but I must choose to be a husband and father.

Here is the point of fundamental difference between male and female. Because the nature is different, the role is different. Though both male and female are necessary for the production of human life, the roles are different. However masculine her hairdo or her dress, a woman can never obscure the fact that it is *within* her that life comes to birth.

That is why the family relationship is inescapable for the female. It was noticeable that when I talked with men about their vocations, family was not mentioned as an issue. The same would be true in talking with young people. But not so with women. Any group of seven or eight women brought together for this kind of discussion would have found family issues unavoidable.

How, then, does a woman choose between marriage and family or a career? What are the standards of fulfillment in each? How may she handle disappointment if the choice she wants is not offered?

The way in which each of you works out for yourself

141

the answers to these questions can be instructed by the basic Christian principle that meaning for your life can only come in relationship. This doesn't mean that motherhood is the only fulfillment of womanhood. Family is one, but only one, set of such relationships. If family is chosen, it must be chosen from the standpoint of Christian love, which considers the happiness of the other as the true road to the self. If family is not chosen or is taken away, then one must choose to set a life's career in the context of relationships with others, these others also loved for their sakes.

There is a certain resentment among women at being treated as a commodity—especially as a sex symbol.

We all ought to be able to understand that, for no one likes to be used as a "thing" for the convenience of the owner. Our contemporary world reacts with enlightened disgust at earlier cultures which held women as chattel-property and often classified them more as animal than human.

No primitive society ever devalued the humanness of woman more than a *Playboy* culture. It has been the repeated story in our time that products which for some reasons, moral or otherwise, are not widely acceptable have been pushed by advertisements showing women enjoying or recommending the products—even down to the abortive effort to sell cigars by this device.

Woman as a sex symbol is not new. Everyone knows something of the history of fertility rites in religion, and it is frequently stated that the world's oldest profession

142

is not that of being a woman, but of being a woman for sale. The Christian response to this is not what has usually been given. Much that has been offered as Christian morality is as dead as the dead gods whose death has been recently announced. But to pronounce as dead what is dead does not mean that all we pronounce alive is truly alive. The new morality may turn out to be an old slavery.

In a world wildly ignorant of the meaning of sex, the Christian response is a faith which has at its center a woman as the supreme sex symbol. Mary the mother of Jesus in the act of giving birth takes the universal role of woman and shows it as the agent of the coming of God into man's life. So that the sexual relationship becomes the point of the joining together of the decisive division of the human race, male and female. This act shows love producing life and life producing the possibility of the presence of God in the world. This, then, is suggestive of the manner in which all divisions in the human race can be mended: by the movement of love into life opened to God.

This physical role of woman explains, then, why concern about sickness and death within the family is a primary thing in women.

The daily life of a woman is more physical than that of a man. (This I would have missed had not the ladies pointed it out to me.) It is the woman who gives her time to the physical aspects of the family—she feeds, teaches habits of hygiene, clothes, cares for the health.

Therefore she is more closely aligned with the area of life where sickness and death are constant possibilities.

Add that to the earlier fact of her larger sexual function, and you begin to see why fear—particularly of those diseases which mar her femininity or bring death through her life-giving female organs—is such a reality.

Here again, the Christian faith calls for utter realism. Fear, sickness, and death are realities which must be faced—not only when they occur, but daily. Our Christian faith takes these facts with such utter seriousness as to call on us all to submit daily to death for Jesus' sake. For the way to handle fear is to go through the event and come out on the other side. We never fear anything that has happened to us if we have survived it and discovered that it can't hurt us.

The experience of the Christian faith is an acceptance of our own kind of death in Christ, in order that prior to our physical death we can live in the freedom of life beyond fear. Not that we can ever, or should ever want, to be freed of concern about these experiences, but even in the day of our great concern we are released from fear.

III

It is this fact of life which gives authenticity to the statement that without reverence for God at the center of life, charm is deceitful and beauty vain. But a woman who has it is to be praised, for her worth is far more precious than jewels.

144

"Hail, thou that art highly favoured [Mary and sisters of Mary], the Lord is with thee." (Luke 1:28 KJV.)

"For he hath regarded the low estate of his hand-maiden: for, behold, from henceforth all generations shall call me blessed. For he that is mighty hath done to me great things, and holy is his name." (Luke 1:48-49 KJV.)

RETIREMENT

CONVERSATION GUIDE

I. The Issues

  A. Time.

    1. Demands from outside the person which have shaped time schedules now drop away. The retired person must plan and schedule his time entirely.

    2. No overall purpose to guide in the use of time.

    3. Sense of guilt in using time on oneself.

    4. Susceptibility to depression.

    5. Balance between hobbies and more "useful" pursuits.

  B. Status.

    1. Status achieved through profession drops away.

    2. Retired person may have trouble defining who he is in the new status.

    3. Changes in financial abilities.

  C. Relationships with others.

    1. Active people don't often think of the need of retired people.

    2. Tendency to spend too much time with a like group; need contacts with young life.

3. Find ways to take the initiative in establishing new relations.

D. Expectations.

1. The difference between what one expects of retirement and retirement itself may be disappointing.

2. The effect of suddenly feeling no longer needed.

3. Decisions must be made about tearing up roots, making new plans, etc.

E. Physical.

1. Less energy.

2. May be actual impairment of faculties which forces early retirement or determines kind of activities possible.

F. Rapidly changing world.

1. How one regards the newness and the swiftness of the world of which one no longer feels a decisive part.

2. Tendency to view events with alarm.

G. Loss of mate or prolonged illness. Plans for retirement may have included a continuation of the marriage relationship, but, without warning, retirement and loss closely accompany each other.

II. Scripture to look at for direction

Psalms 1

Titus 2:2-3

Longevity promised to the obedient: Deuteronomy 5:33; 11:20-21; I Kings 3:14; Job 5:26; Psalms 91:16; Proverbs 10:27; Isaiah 65:22; I Peter 3:10-12

Vigorous age: Deuteronomy 34:7; Joshua 14:11; Luke
2:36-37

Feebleness in age: I Kings 1:1; Psalms 71:9; Ecclesiastes 12:5; Hebrews 11:20-22

Gray hairs: I Samuel 12:2; Job 15:10; Proverbs 16:31;
20:29

Dimness of vision: Genesis 27:1; 48:10; I Samuel 3:2;
4:15; Ecclesiastes 12:3

Reverence for elders: Exodus 10:12; Leviticus 19:32;
I Timothy 5:1

STATEMENT OF THE ISSUES
by ARTHUR L. MYERS

Anticipation! Fulfillment! How often our hopes and
plans fail to materialize. So it is with retirement. Seldom
does it bring into being that blissful state dreamed of
when, wearied by incessant demands on us, we long for
the time we can be on our own, to do as we please.

The group of retired members of this congregation
which I represent suggested and discussed many of the
perplexing problems which often confront retired persons. We examined also a number of pertinent scriptural
references.

Out of our thinking and consideration the following
issues emerged as the most important:

1. *Time.* The retired person is now on his own, freed

of restricting schedules. How shall he use this new freedom?

2. *Status.* Usually the retired person is no longer a factor, big or little, in an ongoing group or organization. Just what in this new situation is the retired person's position in society?

3. *Relationship to others.* With whom does a retired person now associate? How does he adjust to the attitude of people still actually at work?

4. *Expectations.* How does he meet possible disappointments and unanticipated situations arising from the retired relationship?

5. *Physical situation.* The impairment of one's faculties or bodily health may change one's plans. The loss of a mate can radically alter one's outlook as well as his mode of living. How is the retired person to adjust to such circumstances?

6. *A rapidly changing world.* Many retired people, pushed to the sidelines as it were and feeling they are no longer vital factors in the struggle for a better world, acquire pessimistic attitudes toward current situations. How can they maintain their Christian faith and contribute effectively toward reversing the trends about which they complain?

Let me repeat theses six issues: time, status, relationship to others, expectations, physical situations, and a rapidly changing world.

Dr. Kirkpatrick will now address himself to these issues. I confidently believe you will receive interesting insights into these problems and helpful suggestions as to how they may be resolved.

SERMON: THE SHADOW GOES DOWN EASILY
II Kings 20:1-11

It is a light thing for the shadow to go down.
—II Kings 20:10 KJV

I

Backward, turn backward, O Time, in your flight,
Make me a child again just for tonight!

We've known that bit of verse all our lives. I never knew until recently that there is more to it. Here's part of the second stanza:

Backward, flow backward, O tide of the years!
I am so weary of toil and of tears—
Toil without recompense, tears all in vain—
Take them, and give me my childhood again!

Neither did I know who had written it until I made some effort to find out—Elizabeth Akers Allen, but now I don't know who she was or is. It's not really much as poetry, but this must be said for her: she has expressed a basic human frustration. All of us, however fine our usual outlook on life, do have those moments when

150

nothing says how we feel quite as accurately as, "Backward, turn backward, O Time, in your flight."

The scripture passage from II Kings tells the story of a great and good king who expressed a universal cry in what he said to one of the greatest of prophets. "It is a light thing for the shadow to go down ten degrees: nay, but let the shadow return ten degrees." He was talking about the sun dial his father had built in the courtyard of the palace. This king, Hezekiah, had just pleaded with the prophet to pray to God to perform the miracle Elizabeth Akers Allen is talking about.

Hezekiah was facing the end of life, and he wanted more time. "It is a light [easy] thing for the shadow to go down ten degrees." "What I want is for God to turn it back ten degrees, give me more time." We all feel this at times throughout life, but coming to the point of retirement faces a person with a special crisis. It is a time when one's Christian faith must bring special help and new strength. For I have observed that many people who can manage the challenges of life well are defeated by the moment and fact of retirement. So I have been privileged to talk at some length and depth with a group of persons who have come to that point. Some have crossed the line; some are just crossing it.

II

This sermon is not a situation in which I preach to persons in a special area of concern, but rather these retired

151

persons preach to all of us who have yet to face the experience. They would say to us that God is adequate for every changing period of life; that a person of faith must be sure his own relationship with God is such that God's adequacy can be brought to bear upon the special needs of any stage in life, including retirement.

Most everyone would agree that it is important to prepare for retirement, but it is surprising how many people fail to do it. This is probably caused by a real reluctance to face the fact of it.

I have known a number of wealthy men who failed to make a will or made a poor one. I'm sure this is an expression of a man's distaste for facing the fact that someday he will not be in charge of his affairs! When one accepts the fact of the need for preparation for retirement, there is a complicating factor: there are no dependable guidelines for this preparation.

The financial problem is one which illustrates the rest. Careful investment made ten years ago in what would seem to provide for adequate retirement support may turn out to be quite inadequate. Frequently plans are based on a continuation of the good health of both partners; then one is taken ill or dies, and none of the planning seems worth anything. It even turns out to be a kind of mockery.

This does, therefore, point toward a deeper level of preparation—not so much for what is hoped will happen, but for anything that may happen. One must develop a flexibility, an adjustability. Perhaps the most valuable asset to take into retirement is the ability to change plans without becoming completely disoriented or unhappy.

This is a word to each of us, at whatever age: the attitudes we build into our character become the largest single factor in our preparation for adjusting to the demands of the new state of retirement.

The whole of scripture describes the followers of God as a pilgrim people. Instead, we try to make of our faith a solid island of security. Such an understandable misuse of faith in our earlier years makes it an unwieldy tool for retirement years.

Perhaps the major area where this flexibility must be brought to bear is in the planning and use of time. For those of us still active in life's vocations, demands from outside us largely shape our time schedules. Anyone who must go to a business every day or anyone who must run a household or go to school has by this fact a very large block of his total time already decided for him.

When retirement comes, this drops away and a person has twenty-four hours on his hands, all of which he must plan himself. And this must be done in the absence of an overall responsibility to help structure the use of time.

There is a deeper complicating factor. We have drilled into us a guilt complex about idleness. Most Americans are ashamed to be caught doing nothing. We've over-exaggerated the dignity of work until we have become shallow people—very busy shallow people. This, then, results in a very defensive, apologetic attitude on the part of many newly retired persons.

When Horace Greeley Smith, retired president of Garrett Seminary, writes about his great joy in sitting quietly, looking out his window for long periods of time and learning lessons from the birds, I know that here is a man who found earlier in his life the true way to use time.

Don't get hung up over the natural aspects of the miracle recorded in II Kings. Whether or not God pushes the sun around in the heavens to suit his pleasure is not the point. The point is that there is a way to lengthen life by turning it over to the wish and will of God.

God lengthens our days by taking the waste out of them and putting depth into them. If two men live 25,200 days each (that's seventy years) and if one wastes 5,000 of them and the other wastes 20,000 of them, though they were born the same day and die the same day one has lived 20,200 of his days and the other has lived only 5,200 of his. In other words, one has lived four times as long as the other.

Who lived the longer—Methusalah or Jesus?

By taking the waste out of our days is meant putting depth and meaning into them. For you see, the more depth we put into the same length, the more we increase the total amount of living.

I've ridden submarines and sailboats. It takes the sub much longer to cover the same distance a sailboat can skim over. Two lives covering the same length—the one with the greater depth will have the greater amount of total living.

Preparation for retirement and the use of time are two problems of retirement with which one's faith helps. Another of almost the same magnitude is the question of one's status, or his definition of himself.

During the time of vocational activity a person is largely defined by that vocation. When the question is asked, Who is he? listen for the answer: "He's the minister at First Church." "He's a banker at First National." "He's a surgeon at Evanston Hospital." "He's vice-president of ————." "She's the wife of ————." "She's the mother of ————." "She's a teacher at ————." "He's a senior at Northwestern." "She's a sophomore at Evanston High." This is the way we answer the question of who we are. We are what we do. But who will you and I be when we are no longer definable by an active vocation?

Status in life carries with it so many concomitants— the price of the house we live in, the car we drive, the ability we have to support causes we are interested in. The financial change in a retired person's life reflects itself at so many points where acceptance was previously determined by the factor of status—which now changes, perhaps radically.

So we ought to begin to examine the factors which we use to define ourselves. This again is where our faith can help us. Because it keeps prodding us to give up false or secondary or temporary definitions of status for the solid, unchangeable fact of our sonship to the Heavenly Father.

Our worth as persons is based on that fact—that we are loved by him—and on our achievements in faith, prayer, love, righteousness, truth, purity, and all the things that never lose their value.

This is necessary because in a time of the loss of the vocational definition of status a retired person must find himself resting on deeper ones than those which do change. This can best be done through relationships with people of all ages and with people of differing interests and attitudes. The retired person must take rather strong initiative in seeing that these relationships develop. To have the courage to take the initiative he must have a very dependable sense of self-definition.

III

This leads to the overwhelming testimony of our preachers for today: the strongest assurances for life in retirement come to them from knowing that God cares.

As we shared meaningful scriptures with one another, this was by far the most dominant note in all of them:

You will not fear the terror of the night,
   nor the arrow that flies by day,
nor the pestilence that stalks in darkness,
   nor the destruction that wastes at noonday. (Ps. 91:5-6)

The Lord is my light and my salvation;
   whom shall I fear?
The Lord is the stronghold of my life;
   of whom shall I be afraid? . . .

156

Wait for the Lord;
  be strong, and let your heart take courage;
  yea, wait for the Lord! (Ps. 27:1, 14)

He will not fail you or forsake you. (Deut. 31:6)

Cast all your anxieties on him, for he cares about you. (I Peter 5:7 RSV)

Even youths shall faint and be weary,
  and young men shall fall exhausted;
but they who wait for the Lord shall renew their strength,
  they shall mount up with wings like eagles,
they shall run and not be weary,
  they shall walk and not faint. (Isa. 40:30-31)

This latter passage from Isaiah always reminds me of Bishop Francis J. McConnell. He was my bishop during the years I served in the Newark Conference as a graduate student at Drew. He led a devotional service at annual conference which he based on this passage. Normally, he pointed out, we expect a writer to begin low and build up to a climax. The prophet here seems to go downhill instead. That is, he starts out soaring like an eagle, drops down to running without being weary, and finally winds up walking and not fainting. In fact, said the old bishop, this is a spiritual progression. It is rather easy, when one has great strength in his wings, to soar. The exhilaration of it keeps one buoyant. It takes more spiritual strength to run without becoming weary, and the ultimate in spiritual attainment is the ability to

157

walk the dull, lonely way, mile after dusty mile, without fainting.

How, then, does one regard the gift of long life? The Scriptures over and over again seem to be saying that long life is the reward for a good life. But then there is the struggle and problem of Job and the crucifixion of Jesus Christ. There are our own experiences and those of people we know. So that we cannot believe that goodness is rewarded with bodily health and long life, and that, conversely, sin is punished with disease and early death. The facts don't stack up neatly that way.

And yet there is a profound level of truth which we must read out of the clear meaning of the scripture regarding the relationship of goodness and long life:

1. Life is a gift from the hand of God. Every day is such a gift, and the greater the number of days given, the greater must be our acknowledgment of the goodness of God to us.

2. Health, wholeness, and life are God's will. Disease, disharmony, and death are enemies to God's will for his children. He offers us the assurance that he can and does overcome them with his will both in this life and beyond. Whatever we may suffer in defeat now, he eventually restores us to true health and eternal life.

3. To live in his presence is to live in such life-giving light as to cast no shadow: "All good giving and every perfect gift comes from above, from the Father of the lights of heaven. With him there is no variation, no play of passing shadows" (James 1:17).

158